Sedgefield in Victorian Times

Life in Sedgefield during Victorian times

Alison Hodgson
Sedgefield Local History Society

Designed & Printed by **hpmgroup** VISUAL COMMUNICATIONS 0191 3006941

THIS BOOK WAS PRODUCED
TO CELEBRATE THE 700 YEARS
SINCE THE GRANTING OF
SEDGEFIELD'S MARKET CHARTER.

LOGO BY CHARLOTTE SOLLY
(HARDWICK PRIMARY SCHOOL)

Acknowledgements

I would like to thank:

Darlington Local History Library where I spent many hours trawling through old newspapers.

Sedgefield Town Council for their support.

My friends and Fellow committee members of the Sedgefield Local History Society for their support and encouragement, particularly Barbara Leo and Carole Reeve for help with early research. Also Peter Reeve, Alison King, Judith Edgoose and Norma Neal for proof reading, especially the latter for her excellent advice.

My husband, Bill, for his support over the years I have been doing this work during which he did the lion's share of the housework while I sat at the computer.

All the people whose photographs I have acknowledged in the book.

Most importantly, the County Durham Community Foundation grant towards the publishing of the book. This money came from the E.ON Butterwick Moor Wind Farm Community Benefits Fund.

I hope I have correctly acknowledged all photos used in the book but if any have slipped through, my apologies. That also goes for any mistakes in the text; I think I have researched everything thoroughly but mistakes often creep in. I would be glad to know of these for future reference.

If anyone has any old photos of Sedgefield which we may not have in our archives, the Local History Society would be delighted to have them or to make copies.

Researching and writing this book has taken up a good deal of the last four or five years but it is something I have always wanted to do and I have thoroughly enjoyed the experience.

March 2012
Alison Hodgson

CONTENTS

Coronation Portrait of the young Queen Victoria by George Hayter

INTRODUCTION

In 1837, at the age of 18, Queen Victoria, only daughter of the Duke of Kent, fourth son of King George III, succeeded her uncle William IV as monarch of the United Kingdom and Ireland. Her reign, still the longest in the history of the United Kingdom, lasting until her death in 1901, saw a tremendous growth in population, wealth and industry in Great Britain, as well as the rapid expansion of the British Empire.

Shortly before Victoria's accession to the throne, George Stephenson and others had invented locomotives capable of transporting goods and passengers. Agricultural produce could now be transported from the countryside to rapidly growing towns, which were often overcrowded and extremely unhealthy. The nineteenth century saw the increasing prevalence of epidemics, cholera perhaps the most frightening, with major outbreaks in 1848-9 and 1854. Many agricultural workers migrated to towns where wages were higher, often living in squalor.

The care of the poor in town and country became an increasing preoccupation with Victorians. Three years before the new Queen came to the throne, the Poor Law Amendment Act of 1834 set up a new system of poor relief. The early years of Victoria's reign saw much unrest among the working classes, suffering unemployment, long hours and high prices. People from all levels of society spoke out against perceived injustices. Radical movements clamoured for parliamentary reform and representation for the working classes, striving to provide education, which would enable working people to take part in decision making. However, entitlement to vote did not extend to all until long after Victoria's reign ended.

These and other events and developments during Victoria's reign, coupled with rapid progress in many aspects of nineteenth century life, naturally affected the town and people of Sedgefield. Historic documents, census materials and newspapers of the time reveal a picture of life in Victorian Sedgefield with all its problems, pitfalls and pleasures.

Extract from 1861-3 OS Map

CHAPTER 1
THE POPULATION OF SEDGEFIELD

AGRICULTURAL SEDGEFIELD
LONG LIFE AND GOOD HEALTH

Even by Victorian times, much had been written about Sedgefield and its enviable position in the countryside. Durham historians such as Surtees and Hutchinson, writing in the 1820s, were followed, in the early years of the new Queen's reign, by others, including Fordyce (in 1857). Victorian County History, a collection of tomes, added to the growing body of information, shedding light on our Victorian past. Most of the parish was on level ground, nowhere rising to more than four hundred feet above sea level. The land, mostly clay overlying magnesian limestone, was generally fertile and well drained by the River Skerne. At this time, land use in the parish of Sedgefield was totally agricultural, despite the fact that the South Durham coalfield lay immediately to the north. No census returns mention any coalminers living in Sedgefield. In the days before public transport, it would have been too far to walk to any of the nearby pits.

For most of the nineteenth century, a third of the land was given over to the cultivation of oats, wheat, barley, potatoes and turnips, the rest mostly pasture. This varied pattern of agriculture enabled Sedgefield to escape the worst of the agricultural depression in the 1830s. In 1821, Hutchinson described Sedgefield as *'one of the finest situations in the county, standing proudly upon a swell of gravely ground, open to every aspect and remarkable for the health and longevity of its inhabitants'*. Doctor Askew, a famous medical practitioner in the eighteenth century, called Sedgefield the *'Montpellier of the North'*, recommending his convalescent patients go there to recuperate. Another early enthusiast declared the world contained only three towns worth living in *'... London, Paris and Sedgefield !'*

At the end of the eighteenth century and probably well into the nineteenth, a large cross in the centre of the village marked the spot where the market was held. Although its precise position is unknown, buildings in the centre of the village green retain the name *'Cross Hill'*. Surtees refers to Sedgefield in 1823 as a *'small, neat market town with*

Looking towards the Cross Hill area of Sedgefield (photo by kind permission of Colin Hewgill)

the appearance rather of a handsome village … considerably elevated above the marshy lands to the south and west'. Although, to this day, many people consider Sedgefield a village, the granting of a market charter in 1312 means that it should properly be called a town.

An agricultural town, Sedgefield escaped many of the economic difficulties affecting urban centres of the country. Although low grain prices and rising population brought problems, the high incidence of pastoral farming meant that local farmers enjoyed a largely buoyant market. The crisis in agriculture was not quite so critical in County Durham as in other rural areas of the country, since the coming of the railways and the existence of many mineral sources provided other sources of employment. In addition, population increase in the north-east of England centred almost totally on industrial centres, whereas that of rural areas like Sedgefield remained fairly stable. However, agricultural areas like Sedgefield suffered particularly during the agricultural depression of the 1830s, heralded in County Durham by a plague of sheep rot, killing countless sheep and causing wages to drop even lower. From this time onwards, rural areas in particular had to deal with an ever increasing number of paupers.

THE CHANGING FACE OF SEDGEFIELD

This study of Sedgefield in Victorian times covers many aspects
of village life, including farming, law and order, education, social
life, health and welfare. Newspapers of the time, most of them now
digitised, have yielded a great deal of information. Census reports of
the nineteenth century, ten yearly enumerations of the population,
have also proved extremely useful in establishing a clear framework,
embellished with details gleaned from other sources.

THE POPULATION OF SEDGEFIELD
ACCORDING TO THE CENSUS, 1841-1891

Year	Population
1801	1184
1811	1307
1821	1268
1831	1429
1841	1345
1851	1362
1861	1808
1871	2048
1881	2601
1891	2816
1901	3167

The number of people living in Sedgefield fluctuated a great deal
during the first half of the century, increasing by only about two
hundred up to 1851. This time of war and depression with a great deal
of unemployment, particularly in agriculture, caused many people to
move away, searching for work. As trades such as the making of lace and
straw hats, found in early censuses, no longer operated profitably, those
involved drifted away to find work elsewhere, often in the bigger cities.

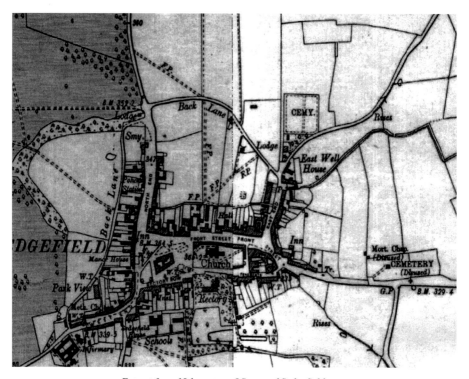

Extract from 19th century OS map of Sedgefield area

CENSUS REPORTS 1841 – 1901

The 1841 census contains little beyond individual names, whereas, ten years later, information includes place of birth, occupation and relationship to the head of the household. An examination of details for Sedgefield reveals the multiplicity of occupations at a time when a community had to be largely self-sufficient. Amongst the predictably common occupation of agricultural labourer, the 1851 census lists several butchers, blacksmiths, gardeners, masons, shoemakers, a couple of drapers and several grocers. The varied needs of an agricultural community were catered for by coopers (barrel makers), farriers, horse breakers, sawyers, a cartwright, a potato dealer, a spade and shovel maker and a saddler. As in all communities, there were several publicans and one brewer and maltster. In addition, there were a couple of carriers, a glazier, a brick and tile maker, a tallow chandler (maker of candles) and a cordwainer (maker of high quality shoes). In 1851, at least a dozen railway workers lived in Sedgefield, many in lodging houses, indicating construction of the nearby railway was in full swing.

Since mothers of more prosperous families would stay at home, caring for house and family, women's occupations, although requiring certain skills, were probably undertaken by poorer females of the parish. As well as a few washerwomen, the census lists seamstresses, dressmakers and needlewomen. Some listed as housekeepers were single women sharing a house with a single man of similar age, therefore likely to be cohabitees, a status not recorded on census forms. Perhaps a job with a higher social standing was that of postmistress. Higher status male occupations included optician, chemist and druggist, machine maker, policeman and inland revenue officer.

INCOMERS AND NEW DEVELOPMENTS

The majority of the population had been born either in Sedgefield or the neighbouring communities, but a surprising number came from elsewhere in County Durham or North Yorkshire, an area which, in those days, included Middlesbrough, Thornaby and parts later designated Cleveland. A sprinkling of people from Scotland included the village optician, Douglas Munro. A watchmaker, Nicholas Ganters from Neustadt in Germany, lived and worked in Sedgefield and a female draper had been born in Gibraltar. Sedgefield farmers were more likely to have come from a different area of the north-east, possibly because young men wanting to set themselves up as farmers, looking for a farm to rent, had to cast the net wider than their own locality.

In the 1861 census, the large number of different occupations persisted, including new additions symbolic of the times. A newsagent and stationer may later have sold copies of the Northern Echo, which began publication on 1st January 1870. Two plumbers were listed and gas fitters were needed from 1854, when gas first became available in Sedgefield. There was also a commercial traveller and a family described as licensed hawkers in drapery. In 1861, only one resident listed himself as an attendant at the Durham County Asylum, Winterton, which opened in 1859. In future censuses the number of employees working there increased considerably.

Possibly thanks to the proximity of the Great North Road, Sedgefield attracted an itinerant population. In 1861, various lodging houses listed a considerable number of residents from Ireland, including a family with small children, although most were single men. Others came from Nottinghamshire, Leeds, Preston (a cotton worker), Suffolk, and Norfolk. A number of Scots made their home in Sedgefield although it is impossible to tell from the censuses how long they remained. In 1861, a great many people lived in the stretch of housing between the Mechanics' Institute (now the Parish Hall) and the Hope Inn, where a system of alleys ran in from Front Street. Poorer families appear to have lived in rather cramped conditions there. A sprinkling of railway workers continued to live in Sedgefield, including a railway inspector, Thomas Hutcheson.

Amongst more affluent families, the household of the Rector, the Reverend Thomas Strong (76 at this time) included his unmarried 36 year old daughter and an elderly unmarried sister-in-law plus a butler, coachman, footman, housekeeper, lady's maid, laundry maid, upper house maid, house maid, dairy maid and kitchen maid. Thomas Davison, a retired army captain, born in Sedgefield, also maintained a large staff to cater for his wife and young family. As well as a housemaid, cook, kitchen maid and butler, he employed a nurse, under nurse and nursery governess. In common with general Victorian practice, most of the staff in both households, not local people, had been placed in service at some distance from their own homes.

1871 – 1901

By 1871 the number of people living in Sedgefield and working in the Lunatic Asylum had risen considerably although far more workers actually lived on site. Very few were Sedgefield born, most coming from elsewhere in Britain, a considerable number from Scotland. Presumably, experienced workers were employed, but many attendants were ex army, apparently considered an appropriate background for working with the 'insane'. The census record for the Asylum lists the numerous staff in full, whereas the 'inmates', who came from all over the north-east of England, are referred to by their initials.

The 1871 census shows three lodging houses in Sedgefield, one in West End, one in Front Street and a third in the Tenements (below the present day social club and at the back of Crispin Court). These cannot have been large dwellings, yet the census reveals a considerable number of people staying there, but not, of course, for how long. A large proportion were unemployed iron workers, originally from Liverpool or Manchester. Since there would have been no work of the kind they were used to in the immediate neighbourhood, perhaps they were en route to another part of the country.

1871 sees the first mention of the job of Toll Keeper. 20 year old John Snowdon, originally from Stokesley, lived with his mother in the Toll Keeper's cottage, somewhere below the Golden Lion. He would keep watch all day for traffic coming in to Sedgefield from the Stockton and Hartlepool roads, exacting the correct toll from the drivers. At this time, people were becoming more vociferous about the state of the roads and newly created parish councils were eager to raise money to effect repairs.

The 1871 census lists a miner, possibly on a short visit to Sedgefield, the nearest pit being about two miles away at Fishburn Colliery. The post office, by now in Front Street where 'Abbraciare' stands today, supported more staff, although the listing of workers (sub postmaster, clerk and two telegraph messengers), shows them all from the same family. Between the post office and the Hope Inn stood the home of Mr Dodds Lewis Vickers, owner of the first Cab and Bus service in Sedgefield. Horse drawn, it must have operated from the yard behind the modern day continental cafe 'Aubergine', on the corner near the Hope Inn.

OVERCROWDING

In 1881, the census indicates areas of Sedgefield with a very high density of population, notably Cross Hill, the Tenements (now known as Rectory Row) and the East End area. In 1871, as well as East End, still in existence today, this included the now vanished Butterwick Street and East Well Street. Of the twelve 'annuitants' living in the Cooper's Almshouses only four were Sedgefield born, others coming from elsewhere in County Durham.

By 1891, the population had grown yet again and there were even more 'incomers' living in Sedgefield. An example of the diversity of place of origin can be seen on one particular page of the 1891 census covering only seven houses in West End. A tally reveals seven people born in Sedgefield, two from Yorkshire and one each from Consett, Hartlepool and Northumberland. Further afield, two people originated from

Leicestershire, two from Northamptonshire, one each from Sussex, Norfolk and Bedfordshire, two from Shropshire, three from Oxfordshire, three from Warwick and four from London. Although this small section may show an unusually large number of people born outside Sedgefield, the complete census reveals a very cosmopolitan society, making a lie of the myth that most people in Victorian times did not venture very far from their birthplace.

The Tenements area in the early years of the twentieth century (photo by kind permission of Colin Hewgill)

In 1891, the most overcrowded areas of Sedgefield remained as before, the Tenements, Cross Hill and East End. More affluent people continued to live in houses below the Mechanics' Institute (now the Parish Hall) and those to either side of the Manor House, now known as Church View, formerly High Row. Resident in High Row, Thomas Lowes was in 1891 registrar of births, marriages and deaths as well as being the local Relieving Officer, responsible for deciding on what money or treatment should be given to the poor. He had taken over both posts from his father, William Lowes, who was still alive and had lived for many years in the house immediately below the Mechanics Institute.

The Manor House, known as such in Victorian times as it is today, even though it never served in that capacity, was home to William Connor from Ireland. A *'clerk in Holy Orders'*, it is not certain whether he was actually connected to the Parish Church, where the current rector was David Falconer. A few doors along lived general practitioner George Sheraton, Sedgefield born and fifty five years old in 1891. Resident at Hardwick Hall, Gustavus Russell aged 27 and still single, later succeeded his father to become the ninth Viscount Boyne.

THE END OF AN ERA

On 11th April 1901, the next census included an assorted group of relatives and others, members of a travelling fair set up on the village green, complete with donkeys, a shooting gallery and a merry-go-round known as a *'Steamhorse'*. Although taken shortly after the death of Queen Victoria in January that year, the inclusion of the 1901 census here neatly brings to an end coverage of Victorian times. It can be difficult to pinpoint either where specific people lived or the correct names of various roads, which could change according to the identity of the census

The gentleman on the horse is John McMorrin, born in Scotland in 1838, licensed victualler of the Hardwick Arms until 1879, when he became a farmer at Town Farm. The unaltered lower windows of the schoolhouse next to the church clearly date this to before the last decade of the century. (from LHS archive)

Rectory Row around the turn of the century (from LHS archive)

enumerator. For instance, the 1901 census names the 'yards' off Front Street, standing in the area between the Hope Inn and the Parish Hall (so-called by this time). Rising Sun Yard seems to have been immediately above the Parish Hall, followed by Office Yard below the Hope Inn. Long gone, these houses and yards must have been situated at the rear of a very old row of shops, now replaced by their modern equivalent. Further down Front Street, just above the Dun Cow Inn, stood Gladstone's Yard, so named after bricklayer Usher Gladstone, aged 55, who lived there with his family. Before the building of a modern house in that position, the old house could be glimpsed, set back from the road.

CHAPTER 2 FARMING

As Victoria's reign began, the effects of the Agricultural Revolution
had become a way of life and Britain was entering a period of rapid
industrialisation. For several years, the number of people working in
agriculture had fallen, as those involved in industry rose. By 1850, less
than 22% of the workforce in Britain was employed in agriculture,
although, in rural areas, the figure was higher. The development of
machinery led to increased productivity, particularly in grain production.
In the 1850s and 60s, John Fowler, an agricultural engineer based in
Middlesbrough, pioneered the use of steam engines for ploughing and for
digging drainage channels. This reduced the cost of preparing farmland
for crops, while allowing land previously uncultivated to be brought into
production. Fewer labourers were needed to work the land, a fact which
had serious implications in rural areas like Sedgefield.

FALLING PRICES AND THE POTATO BLIGHT

In 1847, the Darlington and Stockton Times, describing difficulties in
farming life, recorded that a local farmer recently refused the 26 shillings
per boll offered for his wheat (equal to 140 pounds weight), demanding
36 shillings. The selling price had now fallen to 14 shillings and 6 pence.
The same edition, reporting the record breaking potato crop produced by
Mr William Hallimond, Master of Sedgefield Workhouse, also alerted
readers to potato disease, beginning to be a problem in nearby areas.
By June 4, 1848, potato disease was noted in fields round Darlington.

Potato Blight, which caused havoc in the nineteenth century, began in
Ireland, where potatoes, the staple diet of many Irish people, turned black
and rotten in the ground, their leaves withered. In 1845, only 50% of
potatoes were harvested. The following year, almost the whole crop was
wiped out. Spreading to Europe on trade ships, by 1848, the blight
reached the north of England, although to a less disastrous effect than in
Ireland, where the rural population depended almost entirely on potatoes.
On the 25th April, 1854, the Darlington and Stockton Times reported an
unprecedented dry spell, seriously affecting agriculture in the region.
There was no grass, the oat crop was suffering through lack of rain and
potatoes could not be planted until rain fell.

EVERYDAY LIFE OF AN AGRICULTURAL LABOURER

In 1871, a nationwide survey of agricultural labourers' pay, organised by the House of Commons, recorded that in Sedgefield the average weekly wage for a man was 17 shillings, a woman 6 shillings and a child under sixteen 4 shillings. Agricultural workers living on a farm paid no rent and received free coal, as well as an allowance of wheat and potatoes. *'The Story of our Village'* by Elizabeth Dunn, issued on behalf of the Sedgefield W.I. in the 1950s, throws additional light on the life of a typical farm labourer. At the age of 83, William Gibbon recalls his childhood and youth in the 1870s and 1880s.

House rents were very low, equivalent nowadays to a few pounds; 1 shilling and 6 pence a week for a cottage with no rates to pay. For 2 shillings and 6 pence you could aspire to a 'better' cottage. One of 10 children, William started school at 5 and left at 14, but was often absent, working on the farm. Later in life, as a gardener at Winterton, the large mental hospital on the outskirts of the village, he earned 22 shillings per week. This was riches compared to the £12 per annum paid to young unmarried farm labourers, who were also allowed full board so they didn't have to pay for food. Labourers were paid twice yearly, in May and November, when hiring fairs enabled them to change farms. The system was much the same for females. Farmers were generally good employers and would allow a man to plant three or four rows of potatoes in one of the ready-ploughed fields.

Thanks to William's amazing memory, we know that, in the late nineteenth century, butter was prohibitively expensive at 9 pence per pound. Flour came in 5-10 stone sacks. No margarine was used, but plenty of beef and pork dripping. Bacon was salt cured to last for a year. Many villagers kept a pig. Those that did not could buy a 'flitch' or side of bacon at 2 shillings and 2 pence per pound. The village was 'self contained', most people rarely venturing as far as Stockton, although the carrier's cart was available for a few passengers, mostly farmers' wives taking butter and eggs to market. People without cows of their own went to the farms and bought milk for 1 ½ pence a quart (2 pints or 1 litre). They could buy 16-20 eggs for 1 shilling (five pence). The Bowes family were the oldest farming dynasty in the village.

Travelling packmen came round regularly selling household items and fancy goods, often giving credit until their next visit. The village saw regular visits by itinerant pedlars, knife grinders, gypsies and saddlers.

An occasional highlight, well remembered by William Gibbon, was the arrival of Italians with bears who would dance to their master's penny whistle. There was little emigration from the village as there was plenty of work. Anyone leaving did so for adventure.

DISEASE

In 1867 an outbreak of 'cattle plague' in County Durham called a halt to all cattle shows, including Sedgefield's. This acute and highly contagious viral disease, now known as Rinderpest, causes high fever and other unpleasant symptoms, often leading to death within six to twelve days. Outbreaks in the nineteenth century regularly involved mortality rates of 90%. In September 1871, 27 cases of foot and mouth disease were reported in the Stockton District, but, as yet, none in Sedgefield. In 1891, after a case of anthrax was found on a farm at Foxton, all the cows were destroyed and the area declared infected.

AGRICULTURAL SHOWS

A prime annual event for the farming community, Sedgefield Agricultural Show, held every summer, continues to the present day, with numerous classes for livestock, shown in the open field and several marquees. Thoroughly reported in the local newspapers, speeches on the current state of farming give a good overview of agricultural affairs in the district throughout the nineteenth century. Every year, the show concluded with a lavish dinner provided during the evening. In 1869, Mr G Watson of the Black Lion Inn catered for the event, when the speech given by chairman Mr C H Ford reflected on cattle disease, the main problem for farmers that year. The hay crop had been excellent, although wheat yielded 13% below average. The same speech noted an improvement in the health of Lady Boyne. Lord Seaham replied on behalf of his father, Earl Vane, later 5th Marquess of Londonderry, who declared himself always prepared to advance the interests of agriculture.

In 1870, the show was held in the field belonging to Mr McMorrin of the Hardwick Arms, who provided the meal for 100 ladies and gentlemen. Lord Seaham represented his father once again, while in 1871, with Countess Vane and younger family members, he arrived at the showfield in a carriage and four from Wynyard Park. The speech that year noted the area's escape from the potato blight affecting Ireland.

Held every year during August, most articles in the local press after the event bemoan the poor weather, rain falling on more than half the occasions reported. Sedgefield Show briefly amalgamated with that of Spennymoor, but soon reverted to its original status.

The Newcastle Weekly Courant of September 1900 reported upon a speech given by Lord Londonderry, for once unable to congratulate the community on the condition of agriculture in the area in the past year, as the cold, wet spring had caused a *'barrenness of vegetation and a lack of golden colour in the corn crops'*. Farmers incurred a great deal of expense buying in feedstuffs. The rains of June gave way to July sun, allowing root and cereal crops to ripen well, but, less than six weeks later, the Northern Echo reported a terrific storm over the north of England. For miles, a sheet of water covered fields between Sedgefield and Bradbury. Quite deep in places, only the tops of trees visible, sheep and cattle had suffered terribly.

As well as Sedgefield Agricultural Show, an annual poultry show, inaugurated in 1872, was held at Hardwick Park, with classes for rabbits and pigeons, as well as poultry. On that occasion, the newspaper reported visitors able to enjoy the beautiful grounds, thanks to Captain Davison, current tenant of Hardwick Hall. A favoured few were allowed to inspect the fruit and kitchen gardens, guided by gardener Mr Thomas Harker. After luncheon at the Hardwick Arms, hosted by landlord Mr McMorrin, visitors returned to the Hardwick grounds to be entertained by Redcar and Greatham band. In addition to many social events revolving around the farming year, Sedgefield Ploughing and Hedgecutting Society held an annual competition, awarding prizes in different categories, including 'youths'.

A NEW INVENTION

On the 6th September, 1878, the Northern Echo reported a new American invention, the self-binding harvester, demonstrated at Sands Farm. Two horses drew the harvester which cut the grain, revolving it into a receptacle where two arms encompassed the bundle while a third put the wire round, twisted and tied it. The sheaf was then thrown out by another arm and laid on the ground. One driver performed all this from his seat. The makers claimed the machine would save the labour of five men, leaving a cleaner stubble with no gleanings. Apparently all the spectators

were very impressed, declaring that even a farm boy could operate it.
*'All that witnessed the trial expressed their entire approval of the reaper
and concurred that sooner or later its use would become universal'*.
However, these first self-binding harvesters had a fault, caused by the
wire used to bind the sheaves. Pieces got into the straw and were
swallowed by cattle. Others fell into the wheat itself, giving out sparks
during the grinding process which could cause fire in a mill. By 1880,
a binder using twine rather than wire allowed the harvesting of 20 acres
a day. It is not known whether any Sedgefield farmers invested in the
new machine.

THE MODERN AUTOMATIC, CORD, GRAIN BINDER.

A machine which cuts, binds and carries the bound bundle
into windrows.

THE WEATHER

Successful farming depended upon the weather, a topic of equally great
interest in Victorian times as today. On July 10th, 1852, Sedgefield
experienced a storm of 'unparalleled violence' when, for five hours,
thunder and lightning raged without interruption. The house of Mr
Robert Rickaby of Morden Moor suffered a great deal of damage, a clock
torn off the wall as an 'afterthought', the servant girl stunned but not

seriously injured. Every newspaper edition carried a weather report and forecast, unusual weather incidents from around the country avidly reported. Our current unpredictable climate and concerns about global warming are perhaps not so new.

In February, 1856, for example, the Darlington and Stockton Times quoted weather warm enough for May. In October the same year, the paper reported violent gales. Flooded rivers all over the region destroyed crops and damaged many ships at sea.

In February, 1859, the weather was so mild that cowslips were in full bloom around Sedgefield. On June 2 1860, a storm blew up, causing much loss of life at sea. Locally, many sheep and lambs were lost. Tow Law endured a 'fearful' snow storm.

Extreme weather conditions recurred in 1881, beginning with a violent winter storm affecting the north- east of England, bringing chaos on the railways and great storms at sea. People froze to death. In Sedgefield, snow in many fields was level with the hedges. Later that same year, a violent summer thunderstorm affected all County Durham.

A horse drawn threshing engine used in Pickering, North Yorkshire in 1896. (photo from LHS archive)

The Sedgefield area suffered extensive damage to hay and growing crops, while, in the village, a roof had been taken off a house, the wallpaper stripped by the wind. In October, a terrific gale over the whole area caused considerable damage to property, bringing down a chimney pot at Sedgefield Station. Telegraph wires lay broken and twisted, tall oaks felled, streams overflowed.

CHAPTER 3 HEALTH AND WELFARE

An eighteenth century doctor referred to Sedgefield, with its apparently healthy aspect, as the 'Montpellier of the North', inferring that, by the standards of the time, it was a relatively wholesome place to live. It is almost impossible to gauge the correctness of his judgement, for a stroll around Sedgefield churchyard reveals, as in most areas of England, a high rate of infant mortality and early death. Rural Sedgefield and the surrounding area lay, however, far enough from the edge of the South Durham Coal field to protect inhabitants from diseases associated with mining. The town did have its insalubrious areas, like the Tenements at the end of Rectory Row, where records often show gross overcrowding. Many died of incurable diseases of the day, such as cholera, typhoid fever, smallpox, diphtheria, tuberculosis and influenza.

PHYSICIANS, SURGEONS AND APOTHECARIES

Medical men were divided into three categories - physicians, surgeons and apothecaries. University educated, physicians, considered most knowledgeable about medicine, examined patients, diagnosed diseases and prescribed medications, although they could not dispense drugs. Neither were they allowed to perform surgery, the responsibility of surgeons, who carried out operations, set broken bones and treated accident cases. Without the university education of physicians, surgeons were apprenticed like other traditional craftsmen and considered as such, albeit highly skilled. It was therefore easier to become a surgeon than a physician. As surgeons rarely made enough money by merely performing surgery, they usually acted as apothecaries as well, dispensing their own drugs. Also trained via an apprenticeship, apothecaries made and sold drugs and were legally allowed to dispense medical advice and prescribe medication.

SEDGEFIELD DOCTORS

Dr Henry Ruddock of Sedgefield, for a while medical officer of the workhouse before establishing his own practice in Sedgefield, was both an apothecary and a surgeon. Since the cost of apprenticeship was very high, most apothecaries came from a wealthy background, often the sons of professional men. Women very rarely featured in any of these professions and were commonly found as nurses and midwives.

The medical profession in the nineteenth century cannot be compared to the highly skilled profession of today and many of the procedures would be considered quite barbaric by modern standards. At the start of Victorian times, leeching, purgation and cold water dousing were still common practices, often ensuring that the patients became even more ill. Even when new and more effective treatments were introduced, most doctors were very reluctant to try anything new and stuck to the old methods. Only towards the end of the century were medical training facilities forced to upgrade their standards.

1n 1827 there were four doctors in Sedgefield plus two druggists, one also a farrier. In 1894 only one surgeon, Dr GR Sheraton is listed, apart from those connected to the Asylum. 'The Crooks Bros.' are listed as druggists as well as grocers and Joseph Calvert, another grocer, is described as a 'patent medicine dealer'. Born in 1836 to Ninian Sheraton, a butcher and farmer in Sedgefield, and his wife Jane, Doctor George Sheraton, was a general practitioner in Sedgefield throughout his career. Having qualified both as a physician and a surgeon, the latter at Edinburgh University, a renowned medical training school, he was very well qualified for the time. He lived in a large house to the right of the Hardwick Arms, still resident there in the 1901 census although by then retired. Next door to Dr. Sheraton, in the house now known as 'The Whins', lived Frederick Hunton, a 31 year old general practitioner, who qualified as a physician and surgeon in 1862.

INFECTIOUS DISEASES

The spread of infectious diseases, many of which could kill, was a constant worry in Victorian times. In the 1830s and 40s, in Britain as a whole, there were three waves of contagious disease. The first, from 1831 to 1833, included two influenza epidemics and the first appearance of cholera. The period from 1836 to 42, saw major epidemics of influenza, typhus, typhoid and cholera.

INFLUENZA AND CHOLERA

Influenza, often fatal in Victorian times, left its victims very much weakened in their defences against other illnesses. Whereas cholera mostly affected the poor, influenza affected all classes equally. The first outbreak of Asiatic cholera, at Sunderland during the autumn of 1831, brought in by sea, killed 52,000. The first issue of the Darlington and Stockton Times in 1847 reported cholera, which would eventually reach British shores, steadily advancing through Europe. Spread by contaminated water, its main symptom dreadful diarrhoea, cholera was a disease very much feared in the nineteenth century and had no known cure. People did not realise that it was caused by dirty, insanitary conditions, rife in the large towns. The theory that disease in general was caused by 'miasma' or foul air, dominated all opinion.

On 10th April 1848, a lengthy article attempted to inform people about the first signs of infectious diseases, pointing out that a person complaining of shivering, headaches and weariness, aching of the back and limbs, sickness, loss of appetite and a nasty tongue was likely to be suffering some sort of fever. The suggested treatment was to put the feet in hot water and go to bed, take a mild dose of 'physic' and eat no solid food, only toast and water, tea, barley water or apple tea. If the symptoms continued, a doctor should be sent for. It was important to give nothing 'heating' such as gin. If the illness turned out to be typhus, after the above symptoms would come hot, dry skin and thirst followed by weakness and a 'great lowness' with a heavy dull look of the eyes. It generally lasted twenty one days, required the attention of the doctor and was very infectious but seldom spread if the room was kept clean and airy. 'Rules from the sickroom' were to be observed and chloride of lime spread on the floor.

Cholera was viewed with such great terror that any incidence in Britain or signs of it approaching mainland Europe was reported. The Darlington and Stockton Times of August 1852 again warned about the approach of cholera, apparently devastating Central Europe. By April 18th 1854, 1,300 people had died of cholera in Glasgow. On July 15th 1854, cholera had come to Trimdon in a 'virulent form', resulting in four deaths, with a further thirteen still suffering. Apparently, death had occurred between eight and fourteen hours after the onset of the illness. More deaths were to follow, but by the end of August the disease seemed to have run its course. Although surrounding towns, especially Stockton and Hartlepool, were badly affected, only one death occurred in Sedgefield. In October 1857 cholera had become evident in the Baltic Ports. By August 1858 a new health concern arose, with signs of the spread of diphtheria, a disease previously called 'malignant quinsy'.

Smallpox

A major cause of death in previous centuries, smallpox manifested itself as a rapidly developing rash of numerous blisters. With a very high mortality rate, those who survived were usually permanently disfigured. In 1837-8, one of the worst smallpox contagions ever killed tens of thousands of people, mainly infants and children. On 10th June 1848, Darlington and Stockton Times noted the prevalence of smallpox, drawing readers' attention to the success of vaccination, strongly suggesting its use be made universal.

An injection of cow pox would produce a mild form of smallpox with no danger to the sufferer. First developed by Edward Jenner in 1796, several years elapsed before the practice became widespread. Although vaccination became available, many people shunned the idea, since it was supplied by Poor Law Doctors, thus carrying the association with poverty. Consequently smallpox was not eradicated as quickly as it could have been. As late as 5th January, 1895, the first meeting of Sedgefield Rural District Council, held at the Workhouse, discussed taking action against parents who failed to have their children vaccinated. The Newcastle Courant of July 13th 1883 reported an outbreak of smallpox at Sedgefield Lunatic Asylum. In January, 1884 the Northern Echo reported smallpox in the Sedgefield area. Sedgefield Union, responsible for administering to the poor, was criticised for removing a girl with smallpox to another union in Durham.

The birth of the Isolation Hospital

In 1892, at a meeting of the guardians of the poor, Medical Officer Dr Sheraton reported a case of smallpox found in a lodging house at 'the low end of the village'. The twelve people in the house were forbidden to leave, but the sufferer could not be removed to a suitable place as none existed at the time. Dr Sheraton confined the occupants to the lower rooms, hanging wet sheets soaked in carbolic acid over the doors. Twelve men living in the lodging house were given 3 shillings and 6 pence a week because they were unable to leave the house to work.

Dr. Sheraton suggested procuring two cottages on the outskirts of Sedgefield to serve as a temporary hospital, to become one of the first examples in the country of an 'isolation hospital'. Several years later, as the Victorian era came to a close, moves began to create such a building.

The County Medical Officer of Health agreed to the proposal as long as no cases of smallpox were treated there. The Board Meeting on 25th January 1901, heard that Booth and Lazenby of Durham were willing to sell 5 acres of land for the Isolation Hospital at £1,000. The Board decided to offer them £750. By the next meeting in May, Booth and Lazenby turned down this offer, demanding instead £850 plus costs. The Board agreed to refuse the site and seek another, requesting land from Mr Hamilton-Russell and Lord Boyne. Since no decision could be made, as Lord Boyne was on holiday, by September, 1901 the Board had agreed to buy the original site for £850.

Sedgefield Union.
PUBLIC NOTICE.

At a Meeting of the Board of Guardians of the Sedgefield Union, held at the Board-Room, on Friday, the 23rd day of September instant,

CHARLES GARTHORNE, ESQUIRE, IN THE CHAIR,

IT WAS UNANIMOUSLY RESOLVED,

That in consequence of the appearance of the Cholera in various parts of the County, and in Newcastle, the Union be divided into the following Districts, viz:—

THE SEDGEFIELD DISTRICT, comprising the Townships of Sedgefield, Bradbury, Butterwick, Embleton, Fishburn, Foxton and Shotton, Mordon, Garmondsway Moor, and Trimdon.

THE FERRYHILL DISTRICT, comprising the Townships of Ferryhill, Bishop Middleham, Cornforth, Mainsforth, Thrislington, Chilton and Woodham.

THE BISHOPTON DISTRICT, comprising the Townships of Bishopton, Newbiggin, Little Stainton, Great Stainton, Stillington, Elstob, and Preston-le-Skerne.

That the Elected Guardians and the Medical Officers resident within the several districts, with such other persons as they may think proper to call to their assistance, be constituted Committees for the several districts.

That the Committees for each district be requested to go from house to house, accompanied, when practicable, by the Medical Officer of the district, to inspect and order the immediate Removal of all Nuisances, and to obtain from time to time as accurate a knowledge as they can of the state of health in their respective districts, and to report thereon when necessary to the Guardians.

That where requisite the several Committees provide at the expense of the Union all such articles, and adopt such measures as may be necessary for carrying these instructions into effect.

Any person refusing or neglecting to remove or abate any Nuisance certified as such by the Medical Officers of the Districts, or the Relieving Officer, will forthwith be proceeded against under the Nuisances Removal Acts, for the recovery of the costs and expenses incurred by the Guardians, their officers, or persons employed by them in removing or abating such Nuisance.

THE FOLLOWING PRECAUTIONS AND INSTRUCTIONS,

To be Observed during the Prevalence of Cholera, were approved of, and ordered to be circulated throughout the Union.

1.—All Persons attacked with Looseness of the Bowels, however slight, either with OR WITHOUT PAIN, are most strongly urged to apply WITHOUT DELAY, for MEDICAL RELIEF, to Mr. RUDDOCK, Mr. CLARK, or Mr. SANDERSON, the Medical Officers of the Union, or any other Medical Gentleman within the Union. Looseness of the Bowels is generally the forerunner of the Cholera, and at this Stage it may, in most cases, be readily and at once PREVENTED.

2.—Keep your Houses Dry, and your Windows and Doors open as much as possible. Remove Stagnant WATER, and all Offensive Matter from around your Dwellings.

3.—Carefully observe Personal Cleanliness. Avoid Wet Clothing and Sudden Chills ; keep the Surface of the Body Warm ; and Wear a FLANNEL-BELT ROUND THE STOMACH AND LOINS, as this is found the Best Preventive of the Looseness of the Bowels, which generally precedes Cholera. Expose Bedding and Clothing to the Sun and Air during the Heat of the Day.

4.—Use plain wholesome Food, avoiding Articles of Diet known to produce Bowel Complaints, such as Fruits and Uncooked Vegetables. Especially abstain from Acid Drinks, and FERMENTED AND SPIRITIOUS LIQUORS.

A careful Observance of these Precautions and Instructions will materially tend to ensure general GOOD HEALTH, which is the best Safeguard against an attack of CHOLERA.

ROBERT F. MIDDLETON,

Sedgefield, 23rd September, 1853.

Clerk to the Guardians.

GEORGE WALKER, PRINTER, NO. 2, SADLER STREET, DURHAM.

A public health notice of 1853 issuing instructions on how to avoid Cholera

THE BOARD OF GUARDIANS
OF THE SEDGEFIELD UNION,

being fully sensible of the great benefit likely to arise to the Public, by carrying out the intentions of the Legislature, **especially at a Period when a formidable Epidemic Disease has made its appearance in this Country,** have resolved to carry the provisions of the said Acts into effect, and have directed their Officers to Certify to them the existence of any Nuisance which may come to their knowledge; and they hope to have the co-operation of the Inhabitants generally throughout the Union in the furtherance of so desirable an object.

The Guardians earnestly recommend that whatever Nuisance may now exist in any Parish within the Union be forthwith removed, and they will be glad to receive through their Clerk, Medical Officers, or Relieving Officers, any information relative to the above matter.

BY ORDER OF THE BOARD OF GUARDIANS,
ROBT. F. MIDDLETON, Clerk.

Extract from a 1853 Public Health notice

ACCIDENTAL INJURY

In Victorian times, local doctors performed many services for which hospitals are responsible today. For example, November 1848 found George Pinkham, butler to Captain Baker of Hardwick Hall, returning in a pony and trap with a hamper of goods he had collected from Sedgefield Station. To gain access to the Hall, he passed through Sedgefield, entering Hardwick Park via gates at the junction of West Park Lane and Durham Road. Coming through Sedgefield, the Shetland pony pulling the cart took fright, the cart overturned, the hamper landing on top of Mr Pinkham. Carried to the Hardwick Arms for medical aid, initial fears that he was mortally injured proved unfounded. Recovering sufficiently to be taken to Hardwick Hall, he was later reported weak, but out of danger.

In January, 1852, two railway employees, Jeremiah Taylor and Thomas Atkinson, returning home after work, called in at Mrs Stainthorpe's drinking establishment at Sedgefield Station. At about 7pm, after three pints of ale each, they set off walking home to Mordon, a mile or so along the railway track. Unfortunately, a train of empty coal wagons had just gone through, some coming loose. The engine reversed rapidly, ran into the men and knocked them down. Escaping with a cut to the ear, Atkinson lay insensible for a while. Taylor, found with part of his right leg severed, was taken home, where Dr Ruddock of Sedgefield and Dr Foss of Stockton attended to him. Their 'services were in vain' since he died five hours after the accident through loss of blood, the verdict accidental death.

THE DEATH OF CHILDREN

A great many of the health issues of the day would never have been seen by local doctors due to widespread poverty and inability to pay any fee. Most people in Victorian times could not afford medical treatment, resorting instead to 'home remedies' and advice from well meaning relatives and friends.

On 19 March 1853, the body of a new born baby girl was found in a field at Butterwick. The post mortem, unable to determine whether the child had been born dead or alive, returned a verdict of 'found dead'. If, as seems likely, the baby was born 'out of wedlock', her mother would have been regarded as quite scandalous if discovered. On 23rd February 1861, the Darlington and Stockton Times reported the sudden death of a six month old baby girl, Mary Jane Marshall, daughter of Oswald Marshall, bricklayer. Taken poorly the week before, her mother had given her four drops of laudanum, followed the next day by two spoonfuls of whiskey in sago. The child got worse and died in a fit, the cause of death given as enteritis and inflammation of the bowels.

On 4th September, 1890, it was reported that thirteen months old William Cairns had upset a cup of tea and scalded his chest. A mixture of lime water and linseed oil, bought at Mr Cochrane's shop, was applied to his chest. It later transpired that lime water and aqua fortis had been given by mistake and the child died. A similar incident happened in Sedgefield in May, 1883, when an inquest was opened at the Black Bull Inn in Sedgefield on the body of the infant child of Mrs Jane Watt. The previous Monday, the child being 'very restless and peevish', the mother decided to soothe it with a mixture of weak gin and water, handed to her by the child's grandmother. Shortly afterwards, the child became dangerously ill. When sent for, Doctor Thompson discovered that the grandmother had unknowingly handed over a glass containing a solution of morphia. The child died soon afterwards and the jury returned a verdict of misadventure.

A MISER'S DEATH

Being not too far from the main route north, Sedgefield had its share of passers-by, some of whom might linger in the village for a while. One such came to a sad end, reported in the Darlington and Stockton Times of 13th June 1863. An inquest was held on a man found dead in bed in the lodging house of Francis Cain, who explained that the deceased, known as Elisha, had stayed with him from time to time in the last two years. He earned a small living by selling hymns, songsheets and other small wares.

Complaining of palpitations to the heart, he would not have a doctor, but asked for cayenne pepper. As the landlady had none, the deceased went out to buy some. He returned saying that he could buy nothing less than two pennyworth so, instead, had bought a halfpence worth of ground ginger. The landlady described the deceased as *'a very miserable man who made half-pence worth of coffee last a month and begged for the rest of his food.'* He was found dead in bed with 8 ¾ pence on him. Mr Ruddock, the surgeon, pronounced the cause of death as ossification of the heart. The inquest returned a verdict of 'found dead- died from natural causes'.

SANITARY DISTRICTS

1875 saw the nationwide establishment of Sanitary Districts, based, in rural areas, on the Poor Law Unions. These organisations were responsible for various public health matters such as providing clean drinking water, sewers, street cleaning and clearing slum housing. Such bodies were replaced in 1894 under the new Local Government Act and henceforth were simply called Rural Districts. Regular reports presented to these boards give a clear overview of health problems experienced in any area during the late nineteenth century.

In 1885, for example, the mortality rate was reported 'somewhat below average for the past five years', 108 children under the age of one dying in the Sedgefield Poor Law Area. A bout of severe weather led to more deaths because of complications like broncho-pneumonia. There had been 16 deaths from scarlatina, although, apart from a case in Fishburn the previous week, the incidence of measles was lower than in previous years. With 'only' 7 or 8 cases reported, typhoid was much less prevalent and smallpox had entirely disappeared. Diptheria was prevalent in Stockton and other neighbouring sanitary districts, but there had only been one death in Sedgefield. In 1895, the report recorded a severe outbreak of typhoid fever at the asylum.

The health of people in Sedgefield Rural District suffered badly during the winter of 1899 when Medical Officer of Health, Dr. Gunton, reported, during December, 39 cases of scarlet fever, two of 'continued' fever, one of typhoid and three of erysipelas, a severe skin infection with associated fever. Scarlet fever, so far of the mild type, occurred in every medical district. That winter, a severe influenza epidemic tore through Winterton Hospital, causing great staffing problems.

DRAINS, SEWERS AND PONDS

As well as health matters, the rural sanitary bodies dealt with items relating to sewage and drainage, all of which were duly reported in the press. On the 29th May 1879, the Northern Echo recorded a meeting of the Stockton and Hartlepool Highways Board, under whose jurisdiction Sedgefield lay. The Inspector responsible for Sedgefield's sanitation had asked for attention to be paid to the drain near the Post Office where liquid stagnated in the channel, standing to a depth of five or six inches, causing an offensive smell. Apparently, the drain had always been cleaned out by road men of the Highways Board, who should not have been obliged to do so.

Also, at both the east and west ends of Sedgefield, all liquid from the dwelling houses was emptying into surface drains on the highway, stagnating to a depth of two or three inches, the smell 'abominable and injurious to health.' Two or three men were employed to clean the drains every Saturday, at a cost of £20 per annum The Rural Sanitary Board meeting on 26th August 1887 heard concerns about the foul smell from an open ditch at Stockton Lane sewer outlet, which passed through Lord Boyne's land. By the time of the next meeting, a month later, three hundred yards of new sewer and a new tank had been authorised, the latter to be placed on waste land at the side of the highway.

In October 1888, sewer gas was reported escaping from a grating in the village. This grating was replaced with a solid top. At the August meeting in 1895, concern was evident for the growing insanitary state of the Almshouses, the Sanitary Board urged to proceed at once with repairs. They clearly agreed, as, at their meeting in April 1896, the Board approved recent improvements to the almshouses, with the proviso that the toilet seats should have been hinged. A meeting in 1895 recommended the pond at North End be filled in, since it was filthy. After discussion, it was decided the pond be cleared out instead. In 1896, attention focused on the Cross Hill Hotel, where an inspection had discovered the old walls very dangerous, requiring urgent action to stabilise them.

THE ARRIVAL OF PIPED WATER

As the century neared its end, Sedgefield still relied on water from wells. Several public pumps served the people of the village, amongst them the recently restored pump standing today on the village green. Many houses had their own pumps or wells in their gardens, the largest giving its name to East Well Farm. In the southern part of the village, the spring in Spring Lane gave an adequate supply of water. The Northern Echo of 10th July 1896 reported the nuisance caused by water from the pumps at the lower end of the village running across the street. A letter was to be written to the District Council.

A view along East End around the turn of the century showing one of the water pumps. East Well Farm is in the background. (picture by permission of Colin Hewgill)

In 1899 the County Medical Officer reported the water supply in Sedgefield unsatisfactory and deficient. The wells were so situated that they were liable to pollution, a tendency which increased during the recent spell of dry weather. The situation was complicated by the multitude of adjoining water authority areas, but eventually the Water Company agreed to lay a pipe up to the edge of their boundary, on condition that the District continue the pipe on to the centre of Sedgefield. The cost would be £1,270.

A few weeks later, a further meeting firmly reiterated the need to update the village water supply, involving the deepening and sinking of new wells. New pumps should also be put into place. The cost would be £180 or 4 ½ pence per pound parish rate. As reported to the meeting of the Sanitary Board on 28th December 1900, the new water pipes were completed, the water about to be turned on. People were reminded to let the water run for a while before using it. Before 1895, almost the whole village had earth closets and sewage bins which had to be carried through each house for emptying. There were three septic tanks, one behind the Workhouse in Station Road, one in Stockton Road and one in the Cow Gap field behind the Hardwick Arms.

Looking up West End towards the centre of the village, showing one of the water pumps
(photo courtesy of Colin Hewgill)

CHAPTER 4   ROAD AND RAIL

With the growth of population in the nineteenth century, the state of the roads, often abysmal, had to be addressed. Turnpike Trusts, set up by an act of parliament in the previous century, had powers to collect road tolls for maintaining the highway. The trusts were obliged to provide milestones to mark distances between towns. Tollgates, often accompanied by a tollkeeper's cottage, were set up to control the traffic, a set of charges levied according to the size of the vehicle. Sedgefield's tollgate, just below the site of the Golden Lion, covered access to the Stockton Road.

By the early Victorian era, tollgates, often operating inefficiently and corruptly, were regarded as a barrier to the free flow of trade. Generally hated, the arrival of railways sounded the death knell for tollgates. Many trusts foundered, others merged. When a trust ended there was often great jubilation, the gates thrown open. Turnpike Trusts in their time, however, had done a good job, creating a decent road framework across the country. Many features of the system, such as milestones and tollhouses, survive as a reminder of that era. By the 1870s, Parliament began closing trusts in such a way that an unacceptable financial burden did not fall on local authorities. The 1888 Local Government Act gave responsibility for maintaining main roads to County Councils and County Borough Councils.

POOR STATE OF ROADS AND FOOTPATHS

Sited where roads meet, not far from the Great North Road, Sedgefield could be expected to have well-made highways. However, William Gibbon, interviewed about his young life in the late Victorian period, (in *'The story of our village'*) recalled roads which always seemed either dry and dusty or very muddy.

In January 1870, George Corner, employed by a Stockton lemonade manufacturer, was driving his van from Sedgefield to Stockton, accompanied by George Heald, a greengrocer from Garmondsway Moor. Negotiating a sharp curve in the road, just a short distance from Sedgefield, the horse fell, the van was upset and both men thrown out.

Heald recovered quickly and, with assistance, carried Corner back to Sedgefield, where he died within two hours. A report stated that, at the point where the accident occurred, there was a stone bridge and the road was only 21 feet wide. The night was dark and foggy. Returning a verdict of accidental death, the inquest recommended Durham Turnpike Road Trustees be informed that the road at this spot was insufficient in width, unprotected and very dangerous to the public.

In 1883, the bad state of repair of the Fishburn to Sedgefield road was reported to the Stockton and Hartlepool Highways Board. In 1891, their attention was brought to the very bad state of the road between Sedgefield Station and Sedgefield, with very little provision for foot passengers. It was decided that a proper footpath would be made. The Sanitary Board meeting in October 1900 heard of great pools of water standing on footpaths between Sedgefield and the Asylum, also in a poor state of repair. The Board agreed to properly kerb those footpaths, as well as the path from Sedgefield to the station.

RAILWAY STATIONS AND THE POSTAL SERVICE

With the building of the Clarence Railway in 1833-4, Sedgefield found itself on the Stockton to Ferryhill line. However, Squire Ord, very much opposed to a station so close to the village, insisted it be built nearly one and a half miles away to the west.

During the latter half of the century, horse drawn buses carried passengers from the railway stations in Sedgefield and Bradbury to the Hardwick Arms, Sedgefield's major inn. For a great deal of the century, carriers transported goods, letters and other packages to Durham on Tuesdays, Thursdays and Saturdays. They travelled to Stockton on Mondays, Wednesdays and Fridays, in each case leaving at 7 am and returning the same day. A foot post from Rushyford with letters from all parts, arrived at nine in the morning, returning at two in the afternoon. The Sedgefield correspondent of the Darlington and Stockton Times reported an example of the excellent postal services. A letter he posted from Sedgefield on Friday at 3pm went via Ferryhill to Scarborough with an order for goods, which arrived at Bradbury Station the following day.

PARISH COUNCIL LOOKS AFTER THE ROADS

The 1894 Local Government Act created parish councils responsible for civic duties in rural towns and villages. In 1895, the newly instigated Sedgefield Parish Council wrote to Stockton and Hartlepool Highways Board, protesting at the vast amount of rubbish littering the roadside near the cemetery on the road to Hartlepool. The clerk was instructed to write to the police in order to get them to take action.

Administration of local charities now came under the auspices of the Parish Council, who hired the Mechanics' Hall to ease distribution of bread to charity cases, ensuring that each loaf weighed 4 pounds. On 13th July 1898, the council was informed about the nuisance caused by the smoke and smell from Mr L Daker's tallow works. Again the Parish Clerk was asked to write to the Rural District Board to seek a remedy for the problem.

CHAPTER 5 EDUCATION

Considering that Sedgefield served a rural and largely agricultural population, in a time before compulsory schooling, it is surprising that so many educational opportunities existed. By Victorian times, education in Sedgefield benefited from charity bequests from an earlier era. In his 1782 will, John Lowther left £600, invested for the provision of clothing and education for eight poor girls. In 1790, Richard Wright's bequest of £800 was to be invested for the provision of the same facilities for six poor boys between the ages of 6 and 14. A free Grammar School certainly existed well before Victorian times, endowed with a field of five acres on Beacon Hill. This yielded £5 per annum in 1821, while Howle Hope field brought in £2 12 shillings.

A NEW SCHOOL

In 1826, on the site of a previous schoolhouse, a new school was built, complete with a dwelling house for the master and mistress. A substantial structure, appearing in many photographs taken later in the century, the new school stood on the east side of the Market Square, next to Cooper's Almshouses, opposite the Hope Inn. Whelan's directory states that the cost of building was defrayed by public subscription, many small contributions possibly coming from local people. Principal sums subscribed amounted to £920. £750 came from various trusts and funds, £70 from four local landowners and £100 from Lord Barrington, the Rector, responsible, with members of the vestry, for the appointment of the master. In 1827, all the money subscribed allowed schoolmaster, Richard Lockey, to teach twelve free scholars as well as 40 or 50 fee-paying children. In 1834, the lower part of the school served as a prison for the detention of criminals or the punishment of petty offenders.

EDUCATION FOR ALL

Although many in the early part of the nineteenth century favoured more widespread education, they did not have the backing of either the government or the majority of the people. Education did not become a priority until 1870, with the first Education Act. The vast majority of the working class felt that education was not for them. Child labour was common at this time, most working class families reluctant to give up the meagre earnings of their children.

At the beginning of Victorian times, a proposal to extend educational provision at the time of the 1843 Factory Act came to nothing. Most Non-conformists and Catholics, very wary of a spread in education, feared that any system would be dominated by the Church of England, their liturgical services providing the educational framework, and children taught the catechism.

Many considered the voluntary system of schooling worked well, avoiding government interference. These voluntary schools, of which there were several in Sedgefield, did not have the power or collective influence to construct a nationwide system. As the century progressed, however, feelings began to change and the idea of a more widespread system of education became more popular. As various factory acts restricted children's working hours, so the belief grew that these children should receive a meaningful education. In the second half of the nineteenth century, as social unrest increased, Britain's commercial and manufacturing supremacy began to decline. The perception that other European countries had a better education system led to a feeling that education was a necessity.

The Education Act of 1870, also known as the Forster Act, marked the beginning of the modern educational system in Britain. From this time onwards, voluntary denominational schools could exist side by side with non-denominational state schools. Elementary schools had to be established nationwide, existing schools being incorporated into the system. Although school boards could charge a fee of up to nine pence a week, at first at any rate, those who could not afford to pay would receive free education. All children between the ages of 5 and 13 were expected to attend. With the 1891 Education Act, elementary education became free for all.

PRIVATE SCHOOLS

In Sedgefield, several private schools existed, including a grammar school run by Richard Lockey and Thomas Adamson's private day school. Although he is still listed as running the school in censuses for 1841 and 1851, there is no evidence of where it actually stood. The 1827 directory, several years before Victoria's reign, recorded that both Robert Soulsby and Jane Young ran day schools, while S.A. Ruddick provided a boarding and day school for ladies. The Reverend William Middleton, curate, ran a boarding school at the west end of the village, possibly the same as that which occupied the Manor

House in the middle of the century or, more likely, the single storey building adjacent to it. The Reverend Middleton ran a 'gentleman's boarding school' from at least 1828 until his death in 1834. His children appear to have continued the school for some time, but no mention of it is made after 1858.

In the 1820s and 1830s about one hundred children were educated at the Church Sunday School founded by the Reverend George Lord Viscount Barrington, who taught the children, assisted by his two curates. The Sunday School stood on the site now occupied by Turner's Garage in Rectory Row.

Mrs Strong, wife of the Reverend Strong, Rector at Sedgefield from 1829 to 1863, bought and financed a building in Rectory Row, which began as a mixed school. All pupils paid a fee, with the exception of three boys and three girls, for whom Mrs Strong herself provided money for fees and clothing. These children were known as 'brown coat' boys and girls after the uniform they had to wear. The school eventually changed to boys only, run by a retired naval captain and known as 'Captain Grieve's School'. By this time, the scholars were probably fee-paying since, by 1870, boys attended the Church of England Free Grammar School.

Early Victorians considered education equally important for boys and girls, although girls tended to focus on domestic skills, and were expected to produce fine needlework at an early age. In February 1882, it was reported that the girls' school had reopened, enlarged to accommodate 52 extra children. At the time of the first Education Act, this school catered for girls only, while the boys had moved into premises in the Tenement, known by then as Rectory Row. According to the 1871 census, the school above the almshouses, over the covered mart, was then run by Teasdale Wallbank, a 31 year old certificated teacher, with the aid of his wife, Maria, who also had four young children of her own to look after.

Up to the third quarter of the nineteenth century, two private infants' schools existed, namely Mrs Sanderson's School in the Tenement and Mrs Rochester's School in East End. When they closed down, the covered mart beneath the girls' schoolroom, just above Cooper's Almshouses was taken over, the iron gates removed, and a large classroom created for infants with a staircase leading up to the girls' school. In 1884, the girls' school could accommodate 95, the infant school 84 and the boy's school 120 pupils. 90 boys actually attended and 80 infants. About the turn of the century, Miss Caroline Wilkinson ran a private school for girls in Church View.

The photo above shows the schoolhouse next to the church with the ground floor , with large arched windows, at this time being the covered mart. There is evidence that it was sometimes used as prison. A gateway into the church yard can be seen and the village green looks very plain without the trees planted at the close of the century. (photo by kind permission of Dave Nicholson)

This photograph clearly shows the schoolhouse on the left hand side of the church. The lower floor of the building has been converted from the large arched windows of the covered mart. This was done in the last years of the century. The young trees seen here were planted around 1897/8. On the extreme left is Fletcher's drapers shop, which continued to exist in Sedgefield until recent years. (photo by kind permission of Colin Hewgill)

CHAPTER 6 LAW AND ORDER

THE BEGINNING OF THE POLICE FORCE

Before Victorian times, no official police force existed anywhere in the country. In some areas, the local community funded well-organised groups of private watchmen, while others had a much more haphazard system and some virtually nothing. Home Secretary, Sir Robert Peel promoted the Metropolitan Police Act of 1829, giving rise to popular early nicknames for policemen - 'bobbies' or 'peelers'. Established in London in the first instance, a body of men was employed to act in a preventative role, a deterrent to crime and disorder, a successful model soon copied elsewhere in the country and other parts of the world. The County Police Act of 1839 created provincial forces, Durham Constabulary being one of the first.

Early Victorian policemen worked seven days a week with only five days of unpaid holiday in a year, receiving a weekly salary of £1. Strict control

A modern photo of the Victorian purpose built Police Station

on their lives meant that they were not allowed to vote, marry without permission or even have meals with anyone from the civilian population They were also required to wear uniform at all times, even when off duty. There does not appear to have been any problem in recruiting men to serve as police officers, since the job would be regarded with respect in the community. A purpose built, very sturdy police station, erected in Sedgefield during Victorian times, continues to serve that function to the present day.

NEWSPAPER COVERAGE OF CRIME

The Victorian press regularly reported salacious or bloodthirsty occurrences, repeated in numerous newspapers throughout the country. For instance, an event reported in at least five papers concerned Mr T Hutchinson, an 'eminent railway contractor', who set out to walk from Sedgefield to Mordon, taking a few glasses of whisky at the public house at the station on the way. He then continued his journey along the track, but was found half an hour later, thirty five wagons having rolled over him.

Quite often in these times, events in Sedgefield were reported in newspapers based in areas some distance away. The Preston Chronicle in 1841 reported that a young woman walking from Sedgefield had been stopped by two men who gave her *'the usual highwayman's alternative of 'your money or your life."* She surrendered fifteen shillings, asking for the return of three shillings, a sum she had borrowed from a neighbour. Once the thieves duly obliged, she went on her way. Shortly afterwards, hearing footsteps behind her, she hid for a while, before seeking a nearby cottage, where she examined her money. The three shillings returned to her were, in fact, gold sovereigns. Presumably, discovering their mistake, the thieves came after her in order to reclaim their more valuable coins.

Another young woman did not escape so lightly. In 1877, Jane Dixon, visiting her father in Fishburn, found herself being followed by John Collingwood. Although she made it clear that she did not welcome his presence, he continued his pursuit and allegedly committed the offence of rape.

THEFT OF LIVESTOCK AND ANIMAL CRUELTY

In 1843, George Shaw was charged with stealing corn and eleven geese from John Burdon, shopkeeper, not the landowner of the same name. P.C. Robinson found seven of the geese in a bag under a heap of stones at the defendant's home in Thrislington. Keeping watch until darkness fell, the police officer saw the defendant carrying away the geese. P.C. Robinson identified the birds as those stolen from John Burdon and Shaw received a sentence of six months hard labour.

In 1847, William Arrowsmith and Christopher Fletcher were fined twenty shillings each for killing and taking game on land at East Close House near Sedgefield, belonging to Thomas Barker esquire. Mary Rawlings, an 'old offender', was charged with 'rescuing' cattle being pounded . They were probably her own cattle originally since 'pounding' was what happened to cattle found wandering. The Sedgefield Pound was the walled enclosure that still exists towards the top of Spring Lane. She was fined 5 shillings plus costs. Three men from Trimdon Colliery who 'feloniously entered' a pigeon cott belonging to Mr John Lockey, stealing a quantity of pigeons, were subsequently committed to Durham Jail.

On 3rd March 1849, Fishburn and neighbourhood saw 'a daring night of depredation' when thieves carried off the whole of Mr. Pott's guinea hens and Mr. Newton's geese and a gander. Also stolen were all Mr Senior's rabbits. Mr Nicholson of Holehouse Farm near Fishburn, fearing he may be next, took all of his poultry into the house for the night. Next day, he found every outer door of his property standing wide open. 'No trace of the depredators has yet been obtained'.

On 31st March 1849, thieves stole hens and a cock belonging to Knotty Hill farmer, John Hall. Stationed at Trimdon, P.C. Kirby, on duty nearby at five o' clock on a Sunday morning, noticed two men, heavily laden. Suspecting something, he quickly followed them. *'The rogues, finding their loads too cumbersome, threw them down, which enabled them to make their escape'*, allowing P.C. Kirby to retrieve the stolen property. As both men were well known to the officer, *'it is expected that they will not long escape the punishment they merit'*.

In January 1877, Robert Thatcher, a farm servant, was in custody at Stockton Police Station, accused of killing and maiming two horses belonging to the South Durham Hunt. The horses had had their windpipes cut. The offender had left bloody footprints, of which casts were taken, proving an exact match to the peculiar sole of the defendant's shoes. The same night, a valuable mare in foal, belonging to Captain Davison of Diamond Hall, was stabbed. It was badly hurt, but survived. The accused pleaded not guilty but was remanded for trial and later sentenced to five years penal servitude.

In May 1878, farmer George Farthing sued gamekeeper Robert Hepplewhite for £5, for the value of three sheep worried by his dogs. The defendant claimed he had been looking for his dogs, missing for most of the morning, but was ordered to pay costs.

THEFT, BURGLARY AND COUNTERFEITING

Victorian newspapers reported crimes that today might be considered fairly trivial. For example, in September 1850, Mr Jeremiah Taylor's house at Mordon was entered while the inhabitants were at work, 19 shillings and 6 pence plus a quarter of a pound of tobacco being stolen. No one, as yet, had been apprehended. Other reports covered events which may be considered misdemeanours, rather than crimes. The Darlington and Stockton Times of 2nd June 1860, reported Charles Haley, a joiner, summoned before the magistrate accused by Mr William Gibbon of cutting through his garden because it was his quickest way to work. A small sum was to be paid for the damage.

On 26th April 1862, John Rudd appeared before magistrate Mr C. Bramwell of Hardwick Hall charged with stealing two shillings, two five pound notes and six sovereigns from John Watt at Sedgefield. At an auction, Rudd had been sitting next to the victim, who, discovering his money missing, charged Rudd with stealing it. Rudd walked away, returning a short time later, asking to be searched, presumably after hiding the missing money. Nothing was found at that time, but when the money was later discovered behind a post in a cart shed, Rudd was committed for trial.

In 1869 James Quigley, also known as Godwin, received seven years penal servitude for breaking into a warehouse at Sedgefield Station, stealing a coat, a pair of trousers and a quantity of tobacco. Found wearing the clothes at his lodgings the next day, he had apparently sold some of the tobacco to a fellow lodger.

The Northern Echo of 10th July 1884 reported a spate of counterfeit coinage circulating in Sedgefield. A 'respectable looking young man' John McCauley, resident in Stockton, used counterfeit coins to pay for various items in Sedgefield establishments. He paid a shilling for a gill of beer in the Dun Cow Inn, receiving ten pence ha'penny change. The landlady, Mrs Squire, later discovered the coin a forgery which could be broken in two. The manager of the Black Lion reported that McCauley had done the same in his premises.

In refreshment rooms run by Mrs Elizabeth Robinson, the defendant gave a 'bad shilling' in exchange for a plate of ham. Trying to pass another forged shilling in Mr Wright's grocery shop, the defendant, on being challenged by the proprietor, affected surprise and handed over some good money. By this time, Sergeant Spirit had been informed and he set out to look for the defendant, finding him at Sedgefield Railway Station, where he was charged with 'uttering counterfeit coin'. When searched, another forged shilling was found in his pocket. He averred that 'it was not me', although, on his way back to Sedgefield, he admitted that, on the road between Thorpe and Stockton that morning, he had given a man three shillings for six counterfeit ones. He was remanded in custody.

THE DEMON DRINK

As in modern times, much crime came about as a result of drunkenness. In 1847, a 'tumultuous affray' in the streets of Sedgefield involved William Brown, James Brown, Lancelot Brown, George Todd and Robert Tweedy, who, on 9th October, were bound to keep the peace for six months.

The Evening Gazette of July 1870 reported on a coroner's inquest held in the Golden Lion Inn, Sedgefield, on the death of Mr Robert Robson. A 52 year old carrier operating between Stockton and Durham, that particular week, he had been drinking so much that he was unable to go to work. At three o' clock on the Thursday morning he had got out of bed, telling his wife Elizabeth that he had to go to Durham that day, since he had not worked all week. Rising at about 6.15 am, she found her husband 'in a stupor' on the kitchen sofa, obviously having had a lot more drink. She sent her daughter for a neighbour and for Sergeant Smith who discovered a six gallon bottle of whisky in the back kitchen, no longer full. Mrs Robson declared it had not been in the house the night before.

Neighbour, Lancelot Barron, testified that, at about four o' clock in the morning, the deceased had rapped on his window, holding a glass of whisky and inviting him to 'take a sup'. Barron found the whisky extremely strong, but did not ask where Robson had acquired it and told him to go home to bed. Just before being called to the Robson house, Sergeant Smith had been summoned to the home of carrier Mr Johnson. His warehouse had been broken into and a six gallon jar of whisky due for delivery to Fishburn had disappeared. The sergeant and doctor, along with another doctor summoned from the asylum, stayed with Robson, until his death at 11 o clock. The doctor concluded that even though very little of the six gallon jar of whisky had been drunk, the victim had been drinking all week and that death was due to alcoholic poisoning.

The Evening Gazette of 12th July 1872 reported William Flutor, Teddy Balding, Joseph Crookshoe and Enoch Short summoned by Sergeant Smith for being drunk and riotous in Sedgefield. Alice Charlton, wife of Thomas Charlton of Sedgefield, said that about one o' clock in the morning she heard the noise of men quarrelling in the street, using 'very bad language indeed.' One man was heard to say that he would kill the other. Mrs Scott, landlady of the Nag's Head said that, after the defendants and two others had been in her house, they had gone into the street 'drunk and riotous.' The defendants, Flutor and Short, stated that their behaviour had been caused by being attacked by the other two men. The sentences meted out suggest this was apparently partially believed, since Flutor and Short were fined 5 shillings each and costs, or fourteen days hard labour, whereas Balding and Crookshoe suffered harsher punishment, with fines of 21 shillings and costs or one month's hard labour.

Even in Victorian times, illegal parking posed a problem. In 1874, Sergeant Fawcett charged William Hodgson of Thorpe with allowing his horse and wagon to stand for half an hour in front of a public house in Sedgefield with no one in charge. Denying the charge, the defendant said he was only gone five minutes, but, since he had been convicted of the same offence twice before, he was fined £2 and costs.

The Newcastle Courant of 1877 reported that Mr Robert Tweedy, a carter of goods between Sedgefield, Stockton and Durham, had, while intoxicated, fallen off his wagon between Sedgefield and Stockton.

The wheels had passed over him and he died shortly afterwards. In 1878, accused of firing a gun at a piece of paper attached to a door in Sedgefield, George Mann was fined £1 2 shillings and 6 pence including costs. For being drunk and disorderly later that same day, he was fined £1 4 shillings.

In 1887, a newspaper article entitled 'Riotous Conduct in Sedgefield' related how Henry Mullen, a hawker, had to answer four charges on the same day. For being drunk and disorderly he received a 5 shillings fine with 8 shillings and 6 pence costs or fourteen days in jail. For refusing to leave the Hope Inn when asked to do so by the landlord, he was fined 5 shillings and 8 shillings and 6 pence costs or fourteen days imprisonment. For throwing water, jugs and glasses through the window of the Hope Inn in to the street when the landlord would give him no more drink, the fine was 2 shillings with £1 damages. Finally, after being refused a drink in the Nag's Head and throwing glasses through the window, he was fined 1 shilling with 7 shillings damages and 18 shillings costs. Terms of imprisonment recommended totalled one month.

The Northern Echo of 18th October 1883 reported that Mr James Hanley had been found 'scantily clad' stuck in the chimney of the home of Mrs Barbara Carr at three in the morning. The chimney and some tiles had been damaged. The defendant, having stated that he had had too much to drink and did not know what he was doing, was fined thirty shillings.

LICENSING LAWS AND THE WATERING OF DRINKS

Publicans themselves were not above the law. Licensing hours existed in Victorian time, as shown by the events of 22nd November 1877, when Sergeant Bolskin spotted, through the window of the Dun Cow Inn, three men with glasses in their hands beyond licensing hours, adding that he saw one of them pay for drink. The defendants admitted being present, but said that they had been invited by the landlord for supper. They were each fined 5 shillings each, with shared costs of 14 shillings and 6 pence. Landlord William Alderson was fined £1 and 8 shillings and 6 pence costs for selling drinks within prohibited hours, but his licence was not to be endorsed.

In October, 1877 five licensed victuallers from Sedgefield appeared at Stockton Police Court accused of the adulteration of gin. They were Joseph Tynan of the Black Lion, William Scott of the Nag's Head, Gilbert Irving of the Hope Inn, Mary Scott of the Golden Lion and

William Walton of the Black Bull, situated at the lower end of the village, near where Theakstons stands today. In the Black Lion, investigating officer, Superintendant Bell, asked for a pint of gin, costing 1 shilling and 8 pence. One third of it sent away for analysis was found to be 48% under proof. The defence solicitor pointed out that, since the gin had been bought at 12 shillings and 6 pence a gallon and sold at 13 shillings and 4 pence, there was virtually no profit, adding that everyone watered down gin. The case was dismissed. Such watering down of alcohol seems to have been a regular occurrence, since some of the people in this case appeared a couple of years later accused of the same crime.

In November 1880, Mr W Gray, landlord of the Hardwick Arms, was summoned for selling spirits below the legal standard. Mr Robert Thompson of the Hope Inn was also charged with adulterating whisky, while Joseph Tynan of the Black Lion, who had also appeared in court three years earlier, was summoned for adulterating both whisky and gin. The bench fined each defendant £1 inclusive of costs. Earlier that same year Robert Orton, a farmer from Sedgefield, was found guilty of supplying adulterated milk to the workhouse. A sample taken was found adulterated with 31% water. The defendant's wife, appearing for him in court, was fined £2 with 9 shillings and 6 pence costs.

MANSLAUGHTER AND ACCIDENTAL DEATH

On 9th June 1855, an inquest into the death of Margaret Hood, aged 40, heard that she was struck by a 'close-bed door', presumably the door which shut off the bed found in the living room of most houses. Pregnant at the time, Mrs Hood died two weeks later, after delivering a still born child. A post mortem decided that death was caused by the blow and a verdict of manslaughter delivered. The accused, Lancelot Barron, a labourer of Sedgefield, had at this time, 'eluded the vigilance of the police'. Apprehended a few weeks later, he was charged with manslaughter, to which he pleaded not guilty. Although he had, apparently, been drinking heavily that day, there was no proof that Mrs Hood died as a result of the attack. He was eventually found 'not guilty'.

A newspaper of 18th April 1863, reported on the inquest held at the Golden Lion on William Gibbon, a 45 year old agricultural labourer. On the Saturday evening, he and his son had set off on a horse-drawn cart for the railway at Bradbury on some business for Reverend Stray. Gibbon was 'worse for liquor and drove.' Just past the workhouse, the trotting horse started to slide, Gibbon fell head first out of the cart and the horse galloped away. The son was almost thrown out too, but managed to draw the horse up, returning to find his father moaning. A joiner named Burdon assisted with the removal of the injured man who died shortly after, as a result, according to medical testimony, of breaking his neck in the fall.

A Victorian policeman

CHAPTER 7 ENTERTAINMENT

THE MECHANICS' INSTITUTE

The Victorian age witnessed a developing interest across society in scientific matters. Public lectures by scientists like Michael Faraday extended scientific knowledge to the general population. In addition, the Industrial Revolution created an urgent need for a workforce able to understand and operate machinery rapidly coming in to use in factories.

Mechanics' Institutes, often funded by local industrialists, alert to the benefits of a better educated workforce, sprang up all over the country. Educational establishments, providing working men with an education, chiefly in technical subjects, they also served as libraries, providing an alternative pastime to gambling and drinking in pubs. First established in Scotland in 1823, by the time Sedgefield Mechanics' Institute, later known as the Parish Hall, opened in 1859, there were over 700 institutes in towns and cities all over the UK. Many Mechanics' Institutes went on to become the first public libraries, some the precursors of universities.

In 1834, inhabitants of Sedgefield and the surrounding district supported a 'well-conducted benefit society', consisting of about 240 members. There was also a 'small, circulating library', suggesting an established tradition of 'self-improvement' before a meeting on 15th December 1848 led to the establishment of Sedgefield's Mechanics' Institute . Chairman Mr G.I. Banks, general secretary and lecturer of the North West Union, gave an introductory lecture on 'Mechanics' Institutes, their nature, design and influence'. Mr Lockey, seconded by Mr Lowes, then proposed the motion, carried unanimously, that *'this meeting, having heard Mr Banks' lecture, approves highly of Mechanics' Institutions and deems it expedient that steps be taken to establish one in Sedgefield'*. Forty people indicated a wish to be members, twelve of whom were appointed to a committee to carry out the project. A soiree organised shortly afterwards, held at the Hardwick Inn and attended by 300-400 people, gave a *'cheering indication of the future progress and prosperity of that institution'*. After tea at 5 o' clock, followed by speeches and a performance by the church choir and a violinist, at 7 o' clock, the curate, the Reverend James Steele, took the chair and the meeting began.

It was reported that, within the last two weeks, a house had been taken for the setting up of a reading room, now open to members. One room would be devoted to instruction in reading, writing, arithmetic, geography, English grammar and history. The other smaller room would serve as the library, open every evening from 7- 8pm. 130 volumes of selected works upon 'various branches of science and literature', had been gifted by the Reverend J.S. Strong, Dean of Durham and Rector of Sedgefield, along with various members and friends. The committee did not intend to exclude lighter branches of literature from the library, proposing to acquire, not Victorian novels, but works on various branches of science, agriculture and grazing.

An early photograph of the Mechanics' Institute, later known as the Parish Hall
(photo by kind permission of Dave Nicholson)

Magazines such as Bentley's Miscellany, Tait's, Sharp's and Frazer's would be taken, along with the Farmers' Herald and People's Journal, while newspapers included the Morning Chronicle and the News of the World, probably markedly different from its more recent namesake.

The Reverend James' report was followed by speeches from Mr. G. Linnaeus Banks and others, described by the newspaper reporter, abandoning tact, as rather 'boring.'

By 1850, although not yet in its permanent building, the institute was reportedly going strong, clearly providing for the more affluent sector of the community, with an annual subscription of £20. About 70 members enjoyed free lectures and occasional soirées, which were well attended. The reading room, open daily between 10am and 10pm, contained 700 volumes. By 1856, the library, still well used, contained 376 volumes, 84 added during the previous year. Originally situated elsewhere in Sedgefield, on a site now unknown, the acquisition of a purpose built hall remained the aim. On 7th November 1857, £250 had been raised, half the sum required to build Sedgefield Institute. Subscribers included Henry Pease, M.P., Joseph Pease, Lieutenant Colonel Strong, Mr Ord of Sands Hall and the Honourable and Reverend Luther Barrington M.A. The Mechanics' Institute did not confine itself to the more serious pursuits of life, allowing the use of its premises for lighter purposes, such as a concert held in May 1886 to fund a seaside trip for children of the parish. When, in 1895, the Institute became no longer viable, the Parish Council agreed to take over the premises and all its debts at a cost of £63 4 shillings 6 pence, plus a further payment for the fixtures. By 1899, the Mechanics' Institute was renamed the Parish Hall.

SOCIAL EVENTS

Since people were unable to travel very far afield, social life in Victorian Sedgefield centred on the village itself. The Hardwick Arms was often the social hub, providing, for example, the setting, on 12th January 1850, for St. Edmund's Church choir anniversary. At a celebratory 'soirée', thirty couples danced till dawn, accompanied by Mr Woodham's Quadrille Band. *'Wines and refreshments were of the choicest kind and were served by a liberal hand, reflecting great credit to the most respected host and hostess'*. As many of the population were involved in farming, social events often revolved around the agricultural calendar. Every winter, at least one ploughing match was held on different farms in the area, always followed by a celebratory dinner, such as that in 1856, when the Hardwick Inn supplied *'good old English fare of roast beef, plum pudding and strong ale'*.

An early twentieth century picture of the Hardwick Arms, the hub of village social activity in Victorian times (picture courtesy of Ron Lawson)

The Sedgefield Quadrille Association aimed to cater for the younger age group, albeit of a higher class than most. The Darlington and Stockton Times of 6th March 1858 reported a ball at the Hardwick Arms, attended by 'most of the youthful sons and daughters of respectable tradesmen and farmers', refreshments provided by Mr and Mrs Charlton, licensees of the Hardwick Arms. Thirty couples of 'the youth and beauty of Sedgefield' with the addition of some from Stockton and Durham, danced to the music of 'Mr. Woodham's celebrated Durham Quadrille band.'

In Victorian Sedgefield, membership of St Edmund's church choir opened the gate to many social events, including an annual summer picnic. In August, 1852, Castle Eden Dene provided the backdrop to a picnic in celebration of the marriage of church organist Mr W. Walton, junior. Neighbours and friends also accompanied the bride and groom. After a slight shower, the rest of the day proved pleasant. While some 'rambled to the sea shore', others wandered off to the more 'romantic parts of the Dene'. Later, singing and other amusements were followed by the picnic. *'While the party were seated under a wide spreading tree, the choir sang a few appropriate songs and their united voices harmonised most agreeably with the spirit of the listeners and the beauty of the place'*. Dancing and singing continued until the time came for the journey home.

During the winter months, Sedgefield, in common with the rest of Victorian Britain, often enjoyed occasions designed for social improvement. On 12th November 1859, Captain Lukes of the Durham Militia, a guest of C. Bramwell at Hardwick Hall, gave a lecture on social life in India, entitled 'Under the Punkah'. The talk, held at the hostelry known at this time as the Hardwick Inn, rather than Arms, raised funds for the new Mechanics' Institute which was fast nearing completion.

THE SOLDIER'S RETURN

Great excitement was occasioned in October, 1855 when Lieutenant Colonel Clement William Strong, the rector's son, revisited Sedgefield after serving in the Crimea, where he had fought in the Battles of Alma, Balaklava and Inkerman. 'A handsome sword and a cordial address were presented to him'. During his visit, Lieutenant Colonel Strong mentioned another Sedgefield soldier, also serving in the Crimea, NCO Sergeant Thomas Denton of the 21st Fusiliers, due to return home the following month. A meeting was called and a collection made to mark Denton's distinguished service on the battle field of Inkerman. Richard Middleton Esquire presented him with a silver lever watch, inscribed, with a gold guard chain, and the sum of £5. 'The gallant young soldier was deeply affected'. With two other soldiers, he had rescued a lieutenant from the custody of two Russians who were dragging him away. They also captured the two Russians, but the rescued man was badly injured and later died. The Newcastle Courant, reporting the deed, recorded that Denton's family resided in Sedgefield in 'humble circumstances'.

CHRISTMAS

Until the beginning of the 19th century, Christmas was hardly celebrated in Britain, often not even taken as a holiday. Queen Victoria's reign saw the beginning of traditions which persist today, many attributable to her marriage to Prince Albert. A London illustrated newspaper of 1848 published a drawing of the royal family gathered round a Christmas tree, familiar to Victoria's husband from his childhood in Germany. It was

Queen Victoria, Prince Albert and their family celebrate Christmas from The Illustrated London News of 1848

rapidly copied in nearly every home in Britain. The sending of Christmas cards was a little slower to catch on because, at first, they were quite expensive, but, by the 1880s, Christmas cards had become a lucrative industry. The tradition of decorating the home with evergreen branches now gave way to ever more colourful decorations.

Although an important festival in Victorian times, Christmas was not organised in the commercial way of today. Before Victoria's reign, gifts were exchanged at New Year. As traditions changed people increasingly gave gifts at Christmas, usually modest wrapped sweetmeats or small trinkets. Victorian times also saw the arrival of the customary Christmas turkey, supplanting goose or beef which had previously been more usual. Although carols had been sung before this time, they underwent a tremendous revival, reflecting the Victorian love of musical entertainment. Old carols were resurrected, often given new words. Many favourite carols sung today originated in Victorian times, while Charles Dickens' 'A Christmas Carol', published in 1843, did much to popularise the new idea of Christmas as a family festival.

In January,1892, the Northern Echo reported on New Year's Eve in Sedgefield, generally fairly quiet, with a band of Wesleyan Singers patrolling the streets and singing. The usual Watchnight Service at the church was well attended and the bells rang out to welcome the New Year. At midnight, the Wesleyans erected a Christmas tree 'bedecked with fancy articles, toys etc.', later sold in the Chapel, raising £2-10 shillings for Band of Hope funds. The Northern Echo's 1894 Boxing Day edition described Christmas festivities in Sedgefield, beginning with the annual supper attended by 60 people. Held at the Dun Cow for the Benefit Society, a 'sumptuous repast', served by hosts, Mr and Mrs Vickers, was followed by entertainment. Many songs were sung.

CHRISTMAS IN THE WORKHOUSE
Around Christmas and the New Year, the inmates of the workhouse received quite a lot of attention, possibly to make up for neglect during the rest of the year. In 1894, they reportedly enjoyed a dinner of roast beef and plum pudding and received gifts of fruit, toys, dolls, beer, sweets, apples, wine, picture books and nuts, all sent in by local people. The inmates were also encouraged to play outdoor games.

To celebrate the New Year, they were entertained to, a 'bountiful' tea through the kindness of Mr Robert Hall of Sedgefield, a plumber living in Front Street, and Mrs Dixon of Bishop Middleham. Fruit was donated by Mrs Jane Landreth of Front Street, a widowed farmer who also operated as a butcher. Her next door neighbour, Mr John Giles, a retired farmer, provided money to give each child 6 pence. The dining hall had been 'tastefully decorated' by Mr G Bowes, Master of the Workhouse, and two of the inmates. After tea, the children played games and toys were distributed, while the older people 'regaled themselves' with tobacco. At the close of the event, hearty cheers were given for the Master and the Matron and for all who had supplied the tea and entertainment.

In 1900, to mark the arrival of the new century, the inmates were treated to a meal of rabbit, courtesy of the Honourable Hamilton-Russell of Hardwick Hall. In the evening, after another 'bountiful tea' provided by Mr J Dixon of Bishop Middleham, games were played with songs and dancing, and there was a 'plenteous supply of tobacco and sweets'.

DRINKING

In the Victorian era, the serious drink problem was not helped by the prevalence of so many drinking houses. Victorian morality was very critical of excessive drinking and the Temperance Movement began urging the reduction in the consumption of alcohol. Members of these organisations often took a very hard line and demanded parliamentary acts against the sale of alcohol, although other groups considered gentle persuasion the best method. Since they could not agree on their aims, the movement achieved little.

The Sale of Beer Act, passed in 1854, restricted Sunday opening, but had to be repealed, following widespread rioting. Sedgefield alone supported ten public houses. Trade Directories listed The Black Lion, the Dun Cow, the Golden Lion, Hardwick Arms, the Hope Inn and the Nag's Head, all of which still continue today, as well as the Black Bull, the Red Lion, the Buck Inn and the Tenement Drinking House. The Church of England Temperance Society, formed in 1862, had a branch in Sedgefield. A meeting in the girls' schoolroom on 28th March 1879, chaired by the Reverend R.E.Thomas, the current curate, heard 'various melodies by the Band of Hope Choir'.

DEVELOPING TECHNOLOGY

During the 63 years of Victoria's reign, life in ordinary houses was transformed by a range of technological developments taken for granted today, such as flushing toilets, plumbed-in baths and showers, regular postal deliveries and light fittings capable of illuminating whole rooms. By the end of Victoria's reign, electricity was being introduced into some homes, Cragside in Northumberland being the first house in the country to be lit by electric lamps. However, at the start of the Victorian period, most households relied on oil lamps and candles, either tallow, spermaceti or beeswax. The cheapest, tallow candles, made from animal fat, burned with a smoky flame and stank. Spermaceti candles, made from whale oil, were harder and less likely to melt in hot weather. Just before the Victorian period, candle wicks were improved by being plaited, which eliminated the need for constant trimming and solved the problem of guttering. By the end of Victorian times, the paraffin wax candle, cheap, odourless and reliable, was in most common use. With the discovery of paraffin in 1850, oil lamps could be burned much more cheaply.

Sedgefield social life was helped immeasurably by the advent of gas lighting, enabling social occasions to continue well into the evening. First used in London's Pall Mall as early as 1807, the spread of gas lighting in towns began slowly, before demand became much stronger in the mid 1880s. Gas lit towns became much safer places, the crime rate reduced. The fact that gaslight cost up to 75% less than oil lamps and candles helped to encourage its use throughout the country. Although many people distrusted gas in their homes and resisted its introduction, gas lighting became much more fashionable after its installation in the Houses of Parliament in 1859.

1854 saw the foundation at the end of Cross Street of Sedgefield's own Gas Company, the site of a candle factory in later years. Although this may appear a rather strange sequence of events, gas declined in popularity by the 1890s, considered a thing of the past. However, as most towns in the United Kingdom were not lit by gas until much later, Sedgefield was very much in advance of general progress. The opening dinner of the Sedgefield Gas Company was held at the Hardwick Inn on 1st September 1855, when 27 shareholders and friends enjoyed a 'most sumptuous repast'. Mr J.B. Hodgson presided over a meeting which included speeches and toasts, while, outside, brilliant gas lights were displayed in the shops and inns, the crowning glory an illuminated 'VR' placed in front of the Hardwick Inn 'blazing forth in beautiful style with three hundred lights'.

For most of Victoria's reign, street lighting was not common anywhere in the country but, yet again, Sedgefield was to be ahead of most communities when, on 26th September 1857, *'a few spirited, private individuals at the east end of the town put up and maintained at their own cost lamp posts and gas lights in their own vicinity, hoping they will be adopted elsewhere in the town'*. It is not known how long elapsed before this hope was fulfilled. Towards the end of the 19th century, the tallow factory had replaced the gas works at the end of Cross St. Apparently the factory, all set to expand, ordered expensive machinery which, en route from America, went down in a ship wreck. The loss proved fatal for the Sedgefield candle industry, which disappeared.

Sedgefield, North End.

View along North End showing the newly erected telegraph poles (photo from LHS archive)

CHAPTER 8 HARDWICK HALL AND PARK

The Hardwick Estate familiar to us today was created in the mid 1700s by John Burdon, heir to a coal mining fortune, who acquired the land in 1748 for £10,800. After buying a further parcel of adjacent land, he employed distinguished architect James Paine to create pleasure gardens, the design ensuring a series of vistas rather than a panoramic view of the entire park. The centre piece, a huge lake, was supplied by springs from the Serpentine, another lake, its elongated shape designed to resemble a river. Excess water drained via an ornamental cascade into the Bottle Pond, thence into the river Skerne.

In his 1823 'History of Durham', Surtees stated that *'The chief beauty of Hardwick is its soft silvery lake, an expanse of water covering 40 acres, edged with wood and grassy slopes, sprinkled with luxuriant evergreens'*. The writer continues: *'the place has been infinitely improved by the taste of the present owner by breaking the masses of tall, naked wood and introducing amidst these bare groves an undergrowth of copsewood and hollies'*.

As owner of Hardwick Hall and Park, John Burdon generously allowed the public to visit his pleasure grounds, often conducted by a gardener on the Circular Walk. Designed to offer a succession of visual experiences, the walk allowed views of various 'follies', situated throughout the Park. Constructed in Palladian and Gothic styles, the most impressive, the Temple of Minerva, stood on a hill surrounded by a ha-ha or dry moat.

Hardwick Hall's elevated position to the north of the lake gave an ideal viewpoint of the Park. However, a change in his fortunes meant that John Burdon's ultimate aim, to rebuild the Hall in a much grander style within the park, was never realised. In 1790 he sold the estate to William Russell, MP, who continued improvements, particularly to the East Park. On Russell's death, the estate passed to the family of his sister Emma, wife of Gustavus Hamilton, seventh Lord Boyne. The Boyne family continued as owners right through the Victorian period, but spent little time at Hardwick Hall, renting out the estate, which, frequently untenanted, was left in the care of the Estate Officer and Gamekeeper.

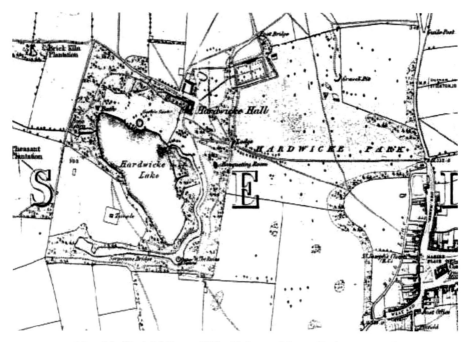

Map of the Hardwick Estate, 1856 – (O.S.map of County Durham – extract)

OPEN TO THE PUBLIC

Even by early Victorian times, despite being rented out to a series of well-to-do people, the estate began to deteriorate, the lake drained by 1873. However, during the 19th century, Hardwick Hall continued to play an important part in the social life of the village, the practice of allowing visitors into Hardwick Park maintained under various tenants.

In August, 1855, a fête was held in the grounds, by kind permission of owner Viscount Boyne and occupier C. Bramwell Esquire. Specially arranged cheap rail trips enabled those from farther afield to attend. Prospective visitors were assured that 'the scenery, pleasure grounds and buildings are exceedingly beautiful and will repay a visit'. With thousands of people attending, the event proved a great success. A portion of the lawn near the Banqueting House was given over to refreshments, with cake, tea, sandwiches and lemonade for all. There followed music, dancing, pony races and a cricket match, while the tenant, Mr Bramwell and his family strolled amongst the visitors. A pleasure boat conveyed Sedgefield Church Choir to the middle of the lake, where they entertained the crowd with some 'favourite glees and songs'.

Engraving showing the lake at Hardwick. (photo by kind permission of the Friends of Hardwick Park)

Also available on that occasion was Hardwick Hall ballroom, the usual venue for the annual ball of Sedgefield Hunt Steeplechase, an event at which, in 1888, the press reported 60 couples dancing from 9pm until 5 o'clock the following morning. The Darlington and Stockton Times of August 1863 announced a forthcoming concert by the 16th Royal Lancers in the 'beautiful and romantic grounds of Hardwick Park'. Once again, by kind permission of Lord Boyne and Mr. Bramwell, the event duly took place on August 11th, proceeds in aid of the Mechanics' Institute. The weather on the day 'delightful', more than 3000 people attended, many coming by train from all directions. At two o' clock, the slope in front of the banqueting House presented a 'thronged and gay appearance, the fair sex having turned out in best summer attire in great numbers'.

VISITING THE FOLLIES

Many visited the Banqueting House to admire the portrait of Hardwick's founder, John Burdon esquire. The newspaper reported in great detail the interior adornments, lavishly describing the lofty room within. Busts of Flora, Sappho, Faustus and Cornelia flanked the Burdon portrait, facing, opposite, the heads of Virgil, Petruvius, Palladio and Inigo Jones, the latter pair noted sixteenth century architects both strongly influenced by ancient Roman and Greek architecture.

The ceiling, beautifully painted in fresco, featured a central portrayal of a feast of the gods, including images of Thetis supplicating Jupiter for her son and of Venus delivering to Juno the Cestus, a girdle affording powers of love. The artist Francis Hayman (1708-1776), a founder member of the Royal Academy, began his career as a scene painter at Drury Lane Theatre. Visitors to the Gothic Seat enjoyed a view of the whole lake, said to cover 40 acres. A relatively new building, the Bath House, with Doric columns in front, contained several fine sculptures of Neptune, Apollo and the Muses. Fresco paintings and further fine sculptures were found in the Hermitage or Bono Retiro.

The Banqueting House (photo by kind permission of Dave Nicholson)

On the hill stood the Temple of Minerva, a square building surrounded by a colonnade of six columns on each side, surmounted by an octagonal dome. Niches contained busts of Homer, Milton, Shakespeare, Ben Johnson and Pope. Inside, above the entrance, a bust of Minerva, to whom the temple is dedicated, surveyed those of Socrates, Plato, Demosthenes, Julius Caesar, Titus, Marcus Brutus and Antoninus Pius, as well as a fine bust of Roman Emperor Trajan, all figures from ancient Greek and Roman history. Paintings by Bornese, father and son, adorned the inside of the cupola,

Minerva herself in the centre. Over the windows frescos portrayed the four cardinal virtues of temperance, prudence, justice and fortitude, while in the corners, paintings represented music, painting, sculpture and architecture. The compartments of the ceiling bore stucco medallions by Cartis, representing the four seasons.

THE TEMPLE, HARDWICK HALL, SEDGEFIELD   N°298.

View of the Temple through the trees (photo by kind permission of Dave Nicholson)

ENTERTAINMENT FOR EVERYONE

For the fête in August 1855, the organising committee had provided 'musical and athletic sports of every description', the first event being a grand musical parade, followed by a balloon ascent. Next came sack racing, for which two prizes were offered. However, only two competitors came forward and, after a 'great many ups and downs', the event was won by an 'old stager', a boy of twelve coming second. Next came a concert by the band of the 16th Royal Lancers, followed by *'pole leaping'* and a half-mile steeplechase. Seven competitors started, but only two finished. One, thinking that the race finished after the last fence, was overtaken by the other before the line. Other events included the 'running high leap', dancing on the green and pony rides. By seven o' clock in the evening, the road to the station was thronged with people going home.

THE LODGE, HARDWICK HALL, SEDGEFIELD   Nº295.

The Lodge at the entrance to Hardwick Park (photo by kind permission of Dave Nicholson)

HARDWICK HALL, SEDGEFIELD.

Hardwick Hall in later years, when it served as a maternity hospital in the 1940s and 50s

The Gothic Tower by kind permission of Dave Nicholson

CHAPTER 9 SOCIAL CLASS

The rich man in his castle, the poor man at his gate
God made them high or lowly and ordered their estate.
Mrs C.F.H Alexander 1848

Victorians had a great sense of belonging to a certain class, nurtured by
the sharp divisions prevailing in those times. Although not encouraged to
'rise above their station', poorer members of the community gave great
respect to middle class families as well as landed gentry. In Sedgefield,
Lord Boyne and Squire Ord were much admired, both considered very
kind and humane. They knew all their tenants and their children by name,
concerning themselves a great deal with their welfare, acknowledging
their responsibility to care for their tenants and workers.

HAPPY EVENTS...

Great interest was always shown in anything concerning the upper or
middle classes. Weddings, in particular, were reported in the press in great
detail. On 12th April 1856, the Darlington and Stockton Times featured the
marriage of Reverend C H Ford and his 'amiable' bride Miss Jane E
Bramwell, who was supported by six bridesmaids. Guests were entertained
with a ball at Hardwick Hall, while the couple departed for their
honeymoon in London. 19th August 1893 saw Miss Wrightson of
Sunderland married to Mr Richard Lowes, eldest son of the superintendent
of Durham County Asylum of the same name. The Northern Echo recorded
a full list of wedding presents, with donors' names. In the evening, a dance
was held at the residence of the groom's father at the Asylum. The couple
honeymooned in Ilkley, Yorkshire.

The Newcastle Courant of August 1882 reported the great welcome given
by the population of Sedgefield to Squire Ord and his bride on their return
from honeymoon. Their horses were unyoked, the carriage and its
occupants drawn by the tenantry and members of the football team, of
which Squire Ord was president. The procession, led by a brass band and
torch bearers, made its way to Sands Hall where villagers had created a
decorative arch over the entrance. The church bells rang throughout.

... AND MISHAPS

Schoolmaster Richard Lockey, despite his reputation for interfering, was considered a prominent citizen, so anything concerning him and his family would be regarded as interesting news. In March 1885, the Northern Echo reported that, while driving in a trap between Green Knowles and Wynyard Station, Mrs Lockey and her daughter were startled by a couple of racehorses in training. The horses ran straight in front of the trap, frightening the nag and causing her to swerve. Mrs Lockey and her daughter were both thrown out, Miss Lockey sustaining injuries to her legs, while her mother injured her back.

Excitement was caused on 12th January 1883 when fire broke out at Squire Ord's residence, Sands Hall, and the neighbouring farm. Despite fire engines attending from Stockton and the lunatic asylum, the barn and its contents were completely destroyed.

Sands Hall, home of the Ord family (Photo courtesy of Ian Spring)

CHAPTER 10 SPORT

THE BALL GAME

Although the Shrove Tuesday Ball Game has long been an annual event in Sedgefield, nobody really knows how it began. In 1891, the Northern Echo repeated the rumour that, after completion of the parish church of St. Edmund in 1256, the builder, representing the tradesmen, sent out a challenge to the countrymen to play a game of football. As today, to begin the game, the purpose-made ball was passed three times through the bull ring on the village green, before being cast to the crowds. The subsequent game ranged over the whole village with the ultimate aim of 'alleying' the ball either in the stream down Spring Lane near the by pass or the duck pond at the junction of West Park and Durham Road. This latter alley is no longer used since the duck pond is long gone.Once "alleyed" the ball would be carried back to the bull ring where it would be passed through three times to end the game. The winner keeps the ball and a new one is made each year.

Always eagerly anticipated, the game was reported in full in the Darlington and Stockton Times and later in the Northern Echo. The 1856 edition stated that *'long before the hour of one o clock, the time fixed for the opening of the Ball game by the Parish Clerk, a strong muster had assembled around the Bull Ring including a good sprinkling of the fair sex'*. For the first hour and a half, the traders had the advantage, keeping the ball in two fields close to the town. When 'the slippery state of the ground and a high close hedge' allowed the advantage to go to the other side, the husbandmen who *'having turned the tide of fortune, by crossing the lane, played the ball with scarcely any opposition across Hardwick Park and ultimately brought her to the alley'*.

The ball game of 1891 was said to have attracted over 1,000 spectators, about 100 joining in the game. At one point, all activity stopped to allow for the passing of a funeral cortege. In 1892 someone broke the rules and made off with the ball to Bishop Middleham, thus bringing the game to an end, while in 1896, the game lasted only forty minutes, when one of the countrymen jumped into the pond with the ball, thus alleying it. That was rather unsporting of him, since, even if chances arose to alley the ball, the game was usually expected to last all afternoon. It was unfortunate that this particular game was so short, since two to three thousand people reportedly attended.

In 1899, flooded fields caused difficulties for the ball game, resulting in 'much flailing around in the water' by the participants, one of whom said 'Aw nivver saw the ball at all, but aw kept kicking watter'. The ball was eventually alleyed by one of the tradesmen in the spring, but was found to have been carried there, not kicked. A group of countrymen went to the house of the player in question, but failed to get in. They called for Sergeant Warwick, who quietly managed to gain access and talk matters over. The ball, soon thrown out into the churchyard, was later alleyed by the countrymen.

The game continues to the present day, attracting people from miles around. Local shopkeepers often take the precaution of boarding up their windows. With no real 'sides', the game nowadays has become more of a 'free for all', enjoyed by everyone who wishes to join in. The ball frequently disappears to nearby villages, visiting various pubs before returning to Sedgefield later in the afternoon, when the ball is presented to the winner, the person who finally alleys the ball.

FOOTBALL, CRICKET AND OTHER SPORTS

Football of the ordinary kind was very popular in Sedgefield and the population seems to have been able to field at least four teams, their results reported in the local papers. In 1893, Sedgefield Rovers were keen players in the Darlington league, with Sedgefield Town another active team. In November 1893, the Northern Echo reported trouble at a game between Sedgefield Rovers and Norton Town, when the referee threatened to punch the Norton goalkeeper for appealing against a decision. After the match, twenty or thirty Sedgefield men lay in wait for the Norton Players at the Nag's Head Inn. Apparently, the presence of policemen averted any further problems.

On 2nd April 1849, Sedgefield Cricket Club was established, enabling its members to 'compete with some of the old established clubs in the County of Durham'. It is believed that the current cricket ground has been in use from these days. In February 1887, a greyhound meeting was held at Hardwick Park, while the Northern Echo of 30th September, 1899 reported Sedgefield Cycling Club flourishing.

It is thought that this photo of the ball game dates from around the turn of the century since the trees planted on the village green around 1897/8 are still young. (photo by kind permission of the late Joyce Wilkinson)

RACING

April 12th 1856 saw the first ever steeplechase, held at Healey House, a farm down Spring Lane towards Foxton. Later the same day, thousands enjoyed hurdle and pony races at Hardwick Park, 'the fog and drizzling rain seeming to be troublesome to only a few'. One of the main events of the sporting season, Sedgefield Steeplechase, was held at varying venues in the district, regularly reported in the press. According to the Northern Chronicle of April 1867, Sedgefield Hunt Steeplechase had taken place over fields belonging to John Bowes and Mr Holmes adjacent to Hardwick Hall. The steeplechase crossed half a dozen ploughed fields and consisted of thirteen 'natural' fences, none being dangerous or difficult.

With being the only race course in County Durham, it is possible that racing took place in Sedgefield before 1732, but 1846 marks the first recorded race, on land belonging to the Ord family of Sands Hall, where National Hunt meetings were held prior to 1867. In about 1870, the old wooden stands were pulled down and it was not until 1894 that the opening

A local cycling group, possibly staff from Winterton. (from LHS archive)

of the new brick grandstand was celebrated with an extremely well attended race meeting. The owner, Mr Ralph Ord, J.P, had, as usual, placed a 'splendid' course at their disposal, thought to be one of the best in the north east.

Two years later, in 1896, the Northern Echo reported an attendance of over 9,000, the Stewards' Stand being filled with 'local aristocracy', including the 6th Marquis of Londonderry and the Honourable Hamilton-Russell.

HUNTING

A local saying of the time, 'to go at a thing like a Sedgefield Hunt', indicates the importance of that particular sport as well as implying speed, energy and attack. At the end of the 18th century, the area around Sedgefield was famously hunted by the Lambton family, their

The Hon, G. Hamilton Russell, Master in 1844
(Picture from "The Sedgefield Country in the 70s & 80s" by Richard Ord (1904)

headquarters by 1804 Sedgefield Racecourse. Ralph Lambton hunted the area until 1838, when he had a bad fall and practically broke his back. From then until his death in 1844 he never rode again, spending the last six years of his life as a tortured cripple.

Mr W. Williamson became Master of Foxhounds in 1838, only giving up three years later because his approaching marriage meant a shortage of funds. In ensuing years, the position was held by many well-known local figures, including the Marquis of Londonderry, William Russell, Colonel Tower, Major Johnson and Sir William Eden, who was master on two occasions. Mr John Henderson and Mr John Harvey served as joint Masters from 1863 until 1872, when Mr Harvey became sole Master. From 1881- 84, the position was held by Mr Ord of Sands Hall, whose family were keen supporters of the Hunt for over a century.

In 1867, due to a reported shortage of foxes in the area, fox cubs were imported from Sweden, which 'in due time will afford sport for the country squires and their pack of hounds'. In November, 1871, infected with a disease called 'dumb-madness', all the hounds had to be

Lord Henry Vane Tempest, a keen huntsman
(Picture from "The Sedgefield Country in the 70s & 80s" by Richard Ord (1904)

Mr. Ralph Ord, Master of the Hunt in 1881
(Picture from "The Sedgefield Country in the 70s & 80s" by Richard Ord (1904)

destroyed, apparently given a dose of prussic acid. After this disaster, resulting in the loss of the whole pack, a countrywide appeal led to many Masters of Foxhounds offering replacement hounds. As a result, the huntsman, Tom Dowdeswell, now had 45 couples of hounds waiting to be trained. The quarters were to be thoroughly disinfected first, but hunting was expected to resume within 14 days. Throughout the 19th century, the kennels were in the grounds of Hardwick Hall, moving to their present site to the north of Hardwick Park in 1922.

In 1872 the Durham Hunt was divided in two, with the South Durham section based at Sedgefield. Mr Harvey, Master of Foxhounds from 1872-78, a tobacco merchant in Newcastle, kept four horses stabled in Sedgefield. In the 1860s, three times a week he would set out from Newcastle at seven in the morning, ride to Sedgefield to go out with the hounds, then ride back to Newcastle. By the late 1870s, he came by train, staying the night at the Hardwick Arms. In the 1870s, after a long day's hunting, Lord Castlereagh, later 5th Marquis of Londonderry, arriving at the Hardwick Inn soaked to the skin, was advised to change. Landlord John McMorrin lent him his best Sunday suit, just arrived from the tailor. On its return, he found a gold sovereign in the waistcoat pocket.

In common with many organisations in Victorian Sedgefield, the Hunt missed no opportunity to hold celebratory meals, often in the Hardwick Inn, so named in those days. On 21 June 1862, for example, the annual dinner of the Hunt was held there, presided over by John Harvey Esquire, who had hunted in the Sedgefield area for 34 years. He referred to the scarcity of foxes but hoped that the future 'would bring good sport'. Several old hunting songs were sung and 'a very lively and amicable evening was spent'.

In February 1886, great excitement was caused when a fox being chased by the South Durham Foxhounds ran into Sedgefield and up to the top of a tall house in East Parade belonging to Mr J Watt. After 'looking around for a few minutes', the fox jumped into the street, running along, pursued by a large number of inhabitants, until it reached a plantation where it disappeared, unhurt apart from being lame after a fall.

CHAPTER 11 RELIGION

THE CHURCH

From its position on high ground, the Parish Church of St Edmund dominates the village in every sense, visible from all directions for miles around. There was probably an earlier stone church in Norman times and a wooden one in Anglo-Saxon years, but the present church, built between 1246 and 1256, is particularly remarkable for its 13th century columns and arches and for the 17th century chancel screen installed by Bishop Cosin.

Until Victorian times, the 90 foot tower, built in 1490, housed the organ at its base. In May 1854, Mr Cahill of the Board of Ordnance came to Sedgefield to make a trigonometrical survey of the district. A framework erected on St Edmund's Church tower rose nearly 7 meters above the parapet walls, thus creating an elevated observatory. Many 'respectable local families', were allowed to climb up and observe objects 30 miles away. Although the church did not acquire a reliable clock until 1897, to commemorate the Queen's Diamond Jubilee, a curfew bell rang every evening, at 8 pm in the winter and 9 pm in the summer. Rung in the form of a hymn tune, followed after a pause by a series of peals to denote the month of the year, the practice of tolling the curfew bell continued until the 1950s.

REPAIR AND RESTORATION

In common with all old buildings, the church needs constant care and renovation, which continued steadily during Victoria's reign as it does today. In 1847, the Newcastle Courant reported that the organ in Sedgefield Church had recently undergone a thorough repair by Mr James Nicholson, an organ builder of Newcastle. Reused for the first time on the previous Sunday by Mr M Redshaw, the organist of St Mary's Cathedral Church, *'the instrument now combines power with sweetness'* The report added that *'among the additional stops introduced with most effect are the cremona, dulciana and open diapason'*.

In September, 1849, Sedgefield Parish Church underwent a thorough cleansing and repairing. A new roof of wood laid under the slates of the south side corresponded with that of the north side, done the previous year.

Interior of St Edmunds Church showing the cosin screen (Picture courtesy of Ian Spring)

The side walls, pillars and centre ceilings were whitewashed, contrasting well with the dark brown of the new roof and the casing of the 'stupendous' organ. Completed within six days, the work cost between £200 and £300. All that remained was the replacement of the dial plate on the church clock and the placing of an additional minute hand. After 33 years of neglect, some of the figures on the clock face were very difficult to read. It was hoped that there might be some money left for this repair. The 1857 edition of the Darlington and Stockton Times reporting the first gas lights in Sedgefield, also recorded the decision to install gas lamps in St Edmund's Church, necessary as there were to be three Sunday services, one in the evening. The cost was borne by a few private individuals in the town.

In December 1863, the Newcastle Courant reported a new stained glass window placed in St Edmund's, accompanied by a brass plate engraved *'from the Bishop and 47 clergy of the diocese to the Reverend Thomas Linwood Strong'*. Resigning after 37 years as Rector of Sedgefield, his son serving as one of the curates, the Rev. Strong was replaced by the Reverend J.P Eden. Also in 1863, various newspapers printed articles about Church wealth, repeatedly describing Sedgefield amongst the richest in the Diocese. On 5 January 1885, the Northern Echo reported that the Reverend John Patrick Eden, Rector of Sedgefield, was seriously

An early postcard showing St Edmund's church – date unknown. (from LHS archives)

ill. He lingered on until May, when he died, aged 75. The article announcing his death reiterated that Sedgefield was one of the richest livings in the diocese, suggesting the opportunity be taken to reduce those benefits to a more suitable level, the residue used to increase smaller stipends. It is not known whether this took place immediately. After the death of the Rev. Eden , Canon Falconer of Stockton took over as Rector of Sedgefield.

THE RECTORY

The living of Sedgefield was very rich, as the Rector was also Lord of the Manor. Often, in the past, the Rector was non-residential, perhaps concentrating on a more 'important' role at the Cathedral, leaving parish work to be carried out by several curates. After fire destroyed the previous house, the large Georgian rectory, built in 1793, by Bishop Shute Barrington and Admiral Samuel Barrington, provided their

The rear view of the Rectory, now Ceddesfeld Hall. Although dating from the early 20th century, this photograph shows a view which will have been familiar in Victorian times. Indeed, it is virtually unchanged in external appearance today. (photo by kind permission of Colin Hewgill)

nephew, Viscount Barrington, Sedgefield's new Rector, a house worthy of his status. Since 1972, part of this building, renamed Ceddesfeld Hall, has been home to Sedgefield Community Association, the other parts two private houses.

An engraving of the interior of Sedgefield church dated 1854

CATHOLIC CHURCH

The Catholic Chapel stood behind a saddler's shop on whose site, at the top of the village, the present Catholic Church stands. The Reverend William Markland was the first resident priest for Sedgefield.

Freemans' Journal of 1 October 1850 reported that, 'to the great gratification of the congregation of the faithful', religious services had been resumed for Roman Catholics in their chapel by the Reverend Robert Suffield who, whilst a student at Cambridge, 'was induced to fly from the Anglican heresy'. This Catholic Chapel fell out of use in 1869.

METHODIST CHAPEL

Although Methodism came to Sedgefield relatively early, there is no evidence of a visit by John Wesley himself. In the 1760s, Jacob Rowell, an evangelist from the Dales, who set up Methodist communities in various parts of the region, regularly preached in Sedgefield.

In the early years of the 19th century, Sedgefield Methodists began to explore the possibility of building a chapel. Most land was owned by the Diocese of Durham or by staunch Anglican churchmen who were suspicious and even antagonistic towards the Methodists. However, in 1812, after buying a plot of land at the west end of the village, they built the first chapel with a library annexe and, from 1827, a Sunday school. With the advantage of a regular meeting place, membership rose to 29, a normal evening service reputedly numbering 100. Unfortunately, records for the chapel throughout the nineteenth century are sparse but it is known that membership fluctuated a great deal and suffered from the fact that many Methodists moved to other areas, some emigrating abroad. By the 1870s, members complained about the lack of visits from a minister, a situation which improved with the reorganisation of the circuit system a few years later.

On 4 April 1857, the new Sedgefield Wesleyan Chapel was opened, a sermon preached there for the first time. A Mr Thomas Barker, gentlemen of North Shields, provided £100 towards the building, the total cost being £365. It is not known whether he had a connection with Sedgefield. Compared with modern standards, the building was very basic, heated at first by an open fire, later by a coke and coal burning stove which gave off huge clouds of smoke. Visiting preachers often could not tell if the streaming eyes and husky voices of the congregation were evidence of their spiritual emotion or the effects of the fire. There was no carpeting and only candles for lighting until gas arrived in Sedgefield.

In October, 1885 it was reported that the Sedgefield Wesleyan Chapel in West End had caught fire. Pews and woodwork were burned when pipes from the stove had overheated. However, early discovery of the fire had prevented much damage and it had been tackled by neighbours with buckets of water. Sedgefield Methodists now have a modern extended church with attached rooms at the north end of the village.

The original Methodist Chapel photographed in recent years, now used as a Scout Hall.(photo from LHS archive)

CHAPTER 12 SHOPS

Information about Sedgefield in Victorian times is available from trade directories and the ten-yearly censuses taken since 1841. However, this first census simply lists names and approximate ages, only occasionally recording occupations, such as licensee of an inn. The 1851 census indicates a multiplicity of shops, 31 in total, many of which would necessarily be very small. Nine blacksmiths were listed, in addition to apprentices and other workers living in the same building. While it is not known whether any blacksmiths joined together in one premises for work purposes, it seems unlikely that the town would have supported nine separate forges.

As well as an optician and two shops serving as chemist and druggist, the 1851 census listed twelve grocers. Although some seem to have operated in conjunction with another trade, such as a bakery or even a draper, it is still inconceivable that they could have operated profitably in such numbers. Yet, by 1861, the number of grocers had actually increased slightly. In 1861, grocer Thomas Alderson offered a shoemaking service, while another, John Cochrane, also operated as a stationer, renamed, by 1871, newsagent. Although a great many shopkeepers were locals, several came from quite far afield, often not staying very long in Sedgefield. In 1861, indicating a much greater degree of mobility than people nowadays imagine to have existed in the 19th century, shopkeepers came from Hartlepool, Darlington, Masham in Yorkshire, Gateshead, Newcastle, Sunderland, Corbridge and Scotland.

By 1871 the number of shops of all kinds has decreased considerably, leaving six grocers and one 'general shopkeeper'. Four butchers in 1851 and 61 had decreased to three by 1871. The Fletcher family ran their draper's shop from at least 1871, when Edwin and Mary Fletcher and their large brood of four sons and four daughters lived above the shop, London House, occupying a prime position at the top end of Front Street. By 1901, Edwin's 25 year old son, also called Edwin, was working as a draper's assistant in the family business. Fletcher's drapers remained in the position shown in the following photograph, serving the people of Sedgefield until the mid 1970s. In 1881, despite the reduced number of shops, two new confectioners had opened, one in West End, the other somewhere on the north side of Front Street. By 1891, a postmaster was listed, a post office specified from 1901 onwards in Front Street, located for many years where children's outfitters 'Abbraciare' now stands.

Possibly taken in the early years of the twentieth century, showing Fletcher's draper's shop on the left and Jordison's grocer's in the centre. (photo by kind permission of Dave Nicholson)

LONG ESTABLISHED FAMILIES

Many other occupations, such as blacksmiths, passed down through the generations, sons often apprenticed to their fathers. Two very long lasting Sedgefield families were blacksmiths.

THE ALDERSONS

In 1841, the founder of one such family, John Alderson from South Church near Bishop Auckland, newly married to a Sedgefield girl, Hannah, had a young baby and was working as a tailor. Ten years later, his family had grown to four boys and he was working as a baker and grocer. By 1861, he is again listed as a baker, his wife a dressmaker; the three youngest boys are at home. By 1871, when the Aldersons were living in West End, one of the boys, by the distinctive name of Israel, had been apprenticed to a blacksmith, while at least two of the other boys followed in their father's early footsteps by becoming tailors.

By 1881, Israel, a fully fledged blacksmith with a wife and five boys of his own, was living next to his elderly parents in North End, on the site of the present petrol station. In 1891, Israel's family had grown to five boys and one girl, most of them, with the exception of one boy, still living at home in 1901. By then, 25 year old George was also a blacksmith. In the previous census, he had been a farm servant at Donnewell Farm, but it is not known how long he had spent there. The Alderson family were to move with the times with the invention of the motor car in the 20th century. No longer blacksmiths, they set up Alderson's garage, which lasted on that same site well past the middle of the twentieth century.

The above photo which probably dates from the end of the century shows the view looking back into Sedgefield from the north along Durham Road. Clearly seen on the right, is the site of Alderson's blacksmith's shop, later a garage. (photo from LHS archive)

Another view of Alderson's blacksmith's shop. (photo by kind permission of Colin Hewgill)

THE HUTCHINSONS

The Hutchinson family were established as blacksmiths even longer than the Aldersons. George Hutchinson, born in Sedgefield, was listed as a blacksmith in 1851, living with his wife Mary (nee Fleetham) two boys and two girls. Still operating as a blacksmith in 1861, aged 72, George's eldest son, John, living two doors away in West End, near the Nag's Head Inn, had also set up as a blacksmith. John had three daughters first, followed by a son in 1863, about the time that his wife disappeared from records, possibly dying in childbirth. This son, also John, was an apprentice blacksmith by the time of the 1881 census. By 1891, John senior had retired but was still living in the same house as his son John, who does not seem to have married until he was about 34 years old. By 1901, he had two sons, the elder also called John.

THE DAKERS

Born in Sedgefield in 1804, his mother an Alderson, Robert Dakers was first listed in the 1841 census as a butcher, married to a slightly older wife and with two young children, Mary and Robert. Ten years later the number of children had stayed the same, unusual for those days. Robert was now listed as a tallow chandler, a diversification quite usual for a butcher, making use of left-over animal fat. Candle manufacturing continued as the family occupation for many more years. By 1861, his son, Robert junior, now aged 23, had joined the business and they were doing well enough to employ one servant. Daughter Mary had set up a grocer's shop, presumably within the same building. By 1871, Robert senior was described as a Master Tallow Chandler. Both children remained living with their parents, Mary still a grocer. Robert junior had married, but in 1871, was already a widower with three young children. Robert senior died three years later aged 70. Only in 1871 does the census record the family living somewhere along Front Street, possibly towards the bottom end near the Dun Cow Inn.

In 1881, Robert junior continued in candle manufacturing with his son, yet another Robert, his apprentice. His only daughter, 17 year old Isabella, was a pupil teacher. His elderly mother and spinster sister Mary lived with them, the latter still operating as a grocer. By 1891, the address had changed to East End, the household diminished to Robert, his son Robert and his sister Mary. The youngest Robert Dakers, now in charge of manufacturing

This photo shows a gathering outside the Golden Lion Inn after the Dakers/Cooper family had taken over as licensees. It is therefore some time after the end of Victoria's reign. (from LHS archive)

candles and living in North End, had married widow Mary Jane Cooper and brought her three children into the household. By 1901, the family had changed direction, taking over as licensees of the Golden Lion, a pub run by successive generations of the family until 1993.

THE GLADSTONES

Another long lasting Sedgefield family still around today were the Gladstones. Born in Sedgefield in 1771 to Robert and Margaret Gladstone, John Gladstone married Isabella Smith in 1792. In 1800, they had a son, John Usher who married another Margaret, producing a son, John Usher Gladstone, born in Sedgefield in November 1823. He eventually became a mason and married Alice Robson around 1843. They had four children, the youngest, Usher, born in 1850. In the 1861 census John Usher Gladstone was doing well enough to be a master mason, employing three men and three boys. Apprenticed to his father when he was old enough, Usher married Jane Wilkinson in 1880, becoming, by the time of the 1881 census, a builder in his own right. By 1891, Usher and Jane had three children, including a 16 year old son,

An early twentieth century post card showing the post office on the left of the photograph.
(photo by kind permission of Dave Nicholson)

another John Usher, apprenticed to his father. They all lived, together with two grandchildren, with Usher's elderly father in a house in Front Street, known, by 1901, as Gladstone's Yard, situated just above the Dun Cow Inn. Usher Gladstone died in 1909 at the age of 59. The old house with a yard in front could still be seen until about twenty years ago.

Looking up Front Street, the Dun Cow Inn on the right of the picture, the long gone Black Bull Inn on the left. (photo from LHS archives)

CHAPTER 13 WINTERTON

With the great growth of population in the nineteenth Century and its accompanying industrialisation, came a massive expansion in the number of 'asylums' throughout Western Europe as a whole. Local Authorities were now obliged by law to make provision for any judged 'insane' and although the prime purpose was to care for these people in the best possible way, the institutions invariably became large and overcrowded with patients suffering a complex mix of medical and socio-economic problems. The treatment of inmates in many of the early asylums was often brutal and was largely based on containment and restraint. Little was done in such asylums in the way of therapy and the medical staff tended to be largely administrators who seldom attended their patients unless they had a physical problem. Understanding of mental illness was very patchy although it was realised that mental illness could take many forms: the term 'schizophrenia' was not to be used for many more years. By the time Sedgefield Asylum was inaugurated, ideas were beginning to change but Sedgefield was to be in the forefront of those institutions aiming to deal with their patients in a more humane and long lasting way.

THE BUILDING OF THE ASYLUM

In August, 1855 it was announced that it had been decided to build a new county lunatic asylum on a site at Far Winterton to the north of Sedgefield. It was to be established under the provisions of the 1808 and 1853 Pauper Lunatics Act as a County Asylum for pauper lunatics. The land was purchased for £4000 and included a house known as Wellgarth Farm. Designed by John Howison, it was to be a 300 bed, three storey corridor plan asylum with a central administrative block, chapel, and superintendent's quarters. There were to be male wards to the west and female to the east with services behind. In the grounds were a stewards' residence, gas works and a terrace of six cottages for married attendants.

The Durham County Asylum opened in 1858 at a cost of £50,000 with eleven men being transferred there from Bath Lane 'Licensed House' in Newcastle. By the end of the first year there were 173 patients although there was accommodation for 300 patients. Wing after wing was added until it housed 750, and after thirty year's existence, the population of the

View of the Asylum (from LHS archive)

'The Gables', the home of the Medical Superintendant – (from LHS Archives)

Asylum had reached 1064. On January 12th, 1861 it was announced that since the enlargement of Sedgefield Asylum, the institute had been getting paupers from Newcastle and it would like to point out that the enlargement had not been for that purpose. A major extension programme between 1875 and 1880 saw the building of a new chronic asylum annexe, a medical officer's block and a recreation hall. A water tower and stables were built and six more cottages for attendants. St Luke's chapel, which could hold 700 people, was completed in 1884.

PIONEERING METHODS OF TREATMENT

From a very early stage in the history of the Asylum, modern methods for treating the mentally ill were being tried; the Medical Superintendent, Robert Smith, (who was appointed in 1857 and remained in post for a further 30 years) was a very forward thinking and progressive man, well

The gentleman with the beard on the front row is the first Medical Superintendent of the Durham County Asylum, Dr Robert Smith M.D. He was appointed in June , 1857 and was to remain in post for a further 30 years. (from LHS archives)

ahead of his time in his attitude towards mental illness. In 1859 he stated that he felt it was far more cost effective to spend one pound in providing amusements and occupations for the patients than in two pounds on surgery although he added that the use of medicine could not be avoided entirely. He said that many cases could be treated successfully with 'employment, exercise, cheerful rooms, music etc…'. A few years later, the same man commented that there was never any need to use either restraint or seclusion since the above regime of keeping the patients amused and occupied seemed to work. It was even reported as far away as in the 'Hull Packet and East Riding Times' in 1869 that a 'Gala Day had been organised for the Lunatics' at Sedgefield Asylum with various sports both for inmates and servants with prizes being awarded. A choir was being formed and led by Mr Hopkiss, the Sedgefield organist, and

The Recreation Room in the Main Building – (from LHS Archives)

there were also plans to form a band. At Christmas time, a large tree was erected that bore gifts for each of the patients, either a necessity or a luxury- 'the wants and ambitions of each having been studied'. Throughout the year, concerts, theatrical performances and balls were held, much to the enjoyment of staff as well as patients.

In 1869 an experiment had been carried out in which fourteen of the noisiest, dirtiest and most destructive women were transferred to a small, comfortable, neatly furnished room under the care of two experienced and intelligent nurses. Very soon, signs of improvement were visible with patients who had never worked before being seen with needlework in their hands. 'The noisy became quiet and the disorderly neat in appearance'. He summarised by saying that if patients elsewhere in the country could be accommodated in such a way, with increased medical supervision, then it would produce better results than *all the restraint, coercion and padded rooms so recently urged in various quarters, to promote their recovery and to increase the happiness of those who can never hope to be restored to their homes and friends'*. He also believed very strongly in providing the patients with a plentiful and healthy diet and said that this was one of the main reasons why the Asylum had a much higher rate of 'recovery' than other asylums in the country. There was, however, some opposition to such treatment and the superintendent commented in 1864 that many of the public were very suspicious and made comments alluding to the paying of taxpayers' money on people who 'knew no better' and were used to a lower standard of comfort at home.

THE STAFF

It was felt important to attract as high a standard of attendants as possible and much was made by the Superintendent of the reasonable rate of pay allocated to staff. In 1873 it was reported that a large room had been allocated to the male attendants as a reading room, which was well supplied by the leading daily and weekly newspapers, magazines, chess, draughts, dominoes etc.. Coffee was also supplied during the winter months and in later years a billiard table was added. The female attendants had a similar room. It would seem that an effort was made to gain members of staff who were experienced in looking after the mentally ill since an examination of the staff lists in the 1871 census reveals that very few were local, with attendants coming from Wiltshire, Lincolnshire,

Ireland and Scotland amongst other places. The three chaplains came respectively from Scotland, Southampton and Bombay.

TRAUMATIC ARRIVAL AT THE ASYLUM

The Superintendent also felt very strongly that patients should not be restrained when they were delivered to the asylum from elsewhere. Apparently, patients often arrived at Sedgefield Railway Station, quite a distance from the asylum, with two attendants (often policemen) and in handcuffs and on many occasions were seen to be walking through the village to the Asylum. It was no wonder that such patients arrived in a nervous and exhausted state. He also deplored that fact that many patients were brought for the first time to the asylum through trickery, presumably being told that they were going elsewhere through mistaken kindness, although often this could also be to spare those accompanying the patient any trouble.

MEDIA INTEREST IN THE ASYLUM

Right from the start , the local media interested itself in anything to do with the Asylum, and its inmates received regular mentions. On 12th October, 1861, for example, it was reported that there had been a 'singular suicide' at Sedgefield Lunatic Asylum when a Thomas Curling had cut his throat with a broken utensil. In the Northern Echo of 22nd September, 1880 it was reported that a 'lunatic' from Sedgefield Asylum had committed suicide while out on an organised walk by lagging behind the others and throwing herself over a wall when they passed a deep quarry, She died after falling 150 feet. This incident was reported in newspapers all over the country.

There is no doubt that the presence of the County Lunatic Asylum on the outskirts of Sedgefield brought many job opportunities to Sedgefield people but there were also some grumblings about the by-products of having the asylum there. A letter to the Northern Echo on 24th March, 1881 stated that due to the large number of suicides and other deaths amongst inmates there was a high demand for Sedgefield residents to act on Coroner's juries. Whereas transport was always arranged for visiting officers to the Asylum, nothing was ever available for those summoned to appear on a jury and they therefore had to walk one mile each day. There was, stated the letter writer, "no justice"!

By 1886, many were concerned that the Hospital was being misused as accommodation for geriatrics. It was pointed out that of those admitted, 23% were over the age of 50 and nearly 60% in a delicate or feeble condition. A report at the time suggested that most of these had just been sent to the Asylum to die. In 1888, the current medical Superintendent commented that *'many patients have been admitted who required no asylum treatment, but only careful nursing which any old woman with average workhouse brains could have bestowed on them'.*

The Infirmary at Winterton (from LHS Archives)

Complaints continued about the overcrowding at the Asylum and the Northern Echo on the 13th April 1888 stated that so many patients were being sent from other areas that it was now urgent that the asylum be enlarged. More and more patients were being conveyed to the asylum in a 'dying condition' and therefore staff were having to cope with medical problems that they had often not been trained for. By 1891 it had already been enlarged 6 times and housed 1150. In 1894 there was accommodation for 1268 inmates and 200 staff. The building covered about 17 acres and the grounds 30 acres with a large farm attached, purchased at the cost of £32,000.

St Luke's Church at the Asylum (photo from LHS archive)

THE CHAPEL

The original chapel for the asylum had been sited in the administration block and was designed to accommodate 200 patients but by 1883 it was no longer big enough. Tenders were invited for a new hospital chapel and the one that was accepted was for £3380 by Jonathon Johnson, a builder from Hartlepool. The finished chapel was dedicated to St Luke and consecrated by the Bishop of Durham on the 3rd October, 1884. It could seat 700 people and congregations of between 100 and 150 were common. A chapel choir was soon formed from local children, for whom a Sunday School was also provided.

The Asylum, renamed Winterton Hospital, continued to be an important centre for the treatment of mental illness throughout most of the twentieth century. Demolished in 1996, a new housing estate now stands on the site.

The entrance to the Durham County Lunatic Asylum. (photo from LHS archive)

Winterton Officers and Nurses 1893 (from LHS archive)

CHAPTER 14 CARE OF THE POOR

Until the passing of the new Poor Law in 1834, Sedgefield had coped with its own poor quite satisfactorily. Rented from the parish for a very small fee since 1759, Sedgefield Workhouse, a rambling building backing on to fields at the east end of the village, provided shelter for the relatively small number of poor people in need of it. Work schemes set up to help the unemployed included the annual purchase of 200 tons of blue stones, divided up into lots of 30 tons and distributed for breaking to men with large families. This spared the family the shame of seeking financial support from the Overseer. Before 1834, the Poor Rate, 'doled out' to those in need, was two shillings a week for a single person, three shillings for a couple with no children and sixpence for each child under ten. A person considered able to work received nothing. While some struggled to maintain a basic standard of living, Sedgefield had few able-bodied paupers, the main category covered by existing Poor Law restrictions. In addition, being a rural area, Sedgefield did not suffer the evils of industry experienced elsewhere.

However, with the passing of the 1834 Poor Law Amendment Act, Sedgefield became the centre of the local Poor Law Union, a much larger area of responsibility. A Board of Guardians was formed to run the Union, staffed entirely by volunteers, who were always in plentiful supply. Nationwide publicity about workhouse conditions and the sufferings of the poor, coupled with the Victorian ideal of service to the community, meant that voluntary work of this kind was considered right and proper. The new Sedgefield Board of Guardians appointed from within a chairman, vice chairman and treasurer, as well as a clerk, Richard Middleton, who received a salary of £40 per annum. Although a part-time position, the clerk was responsible for elections and voting, correspondence, taking minutes of meetings, supervising the accounts and giving legal advice. Not elected annually, clerks usually held the post for a considerable time, often alongside a full-time job, and were held in high esteem in the community.

Of lower social status, the Relieving Officer was responsible for determining who received financial support. Starting on a salary of £70 per annum, this reduced to £50 when the Relieving Officer became eligible to receive a fee for registration of births, marriages and deaths, compulsory from 1837. Sedgefield's first Relieving Officer, William

Eels, held office until April 1842, when a protracted series of allegations finally led to his dismissal for incompetence. Two further men briefly held office before the appointment of William Lowes, who remained in post until his retirement in the 1880s. His family remained in Sedgefield, descendants living in the village until recent years.

OUTDOOR RELIEF

In Sedgefield, in common with the rest of the north of England, most workhouse inmates were old and infirm. A system of out-relief provided for the remainder of the needy, a regular 'dole' of money allowing them to survive outside the workhouse. Under the new Poor Law, relief outside the workhouse was not to be given to any able-bodied pauper and to others only under certain strict circumstances. The choice lay between entering the workhouse under conditions inferior to their everyday lives or coping without aid of any kind. Since bringing such able-bodied paupers in to the workhouse would increase the cost to the Poor Law Union, in the years immediately following 1834 this new stipulation was not enforced. Outdoor relief was allowed in cases of illness, possibly often invented, giving the guardians leave to assist people without the expense of moving them into the workhouse.

However, during the 1840s, the onset of agricultural and industrial depression coincided with a growth in population in the north. County Durham saw an increase of 27% between 1841 and 1845, the second highest in the country. As the number of paupers grew, so the rate burden became higher. Many Poor Law Commissioners in London, ignoring the basic economic situation, believed that previous laxity had caused this situation. Consequently, they prohibited outdoor relief except in certain stated circumstances, urging the rigorously applied principle of 'less eligibility'. The order prohibited outdoor relief to able-bodied persons except in cases of 'sudden need', sickness or infirmity or for the payment of funeral expenses. Relief was also allowed for the first six months of widowhood, also to widows with at least one legitimate child and to families whose breadwinner was in jail or in Her Majesty's Service. Thus, unemployed agricultural or industrial labourers became the main group of people debarred from outdoor relief.

With the passing of the 1834 Poor Law, in Sedgefield, as in the rest of the country, workhouse numbers increased dramatically, most of the additional inmates being able bodied. Farmers, contributing most to the Poor Rate, were keen to limit the number of poor, but, as major employers, they needed to reduce their workforce if conditions warranted, thus adding to the burden of the Poor Rate. Not only did they often have this conflicting responsibility, but farmers were very often the same Guardians of the Poor who had to try and put self-interest aside in considering the welfare of paupers.

Numbers in the workhouse always rose during the winter months due to the lack of employment, falling again in late summer, when harvest time brought plenty of work, usually for men. Jobs suited to female capabilities were more plentiful in spring, but women could then face unemployment until the following spring. As the 19th century progressed, the decline of cottage industries and the introduction of agricultural machinery favoured the employment of men rather than women.

VAGRANTS

Although Victorians generally considered vagrants of a criminal tendency, deliberately choosing to be 'on the move' for most of the year, they were supposed to be offered a night's shelter in the workhouse, before being removed to their parish of settlement, their birthplace, at the cost of the complaining parish. Sedgefield's location, close to a main road linking south and north, provided an ideal stopping point. In the 1820s and 30s, the tremendous increase in the number of such travelling paupers, coupled with the costs of returning them, added considerably to the taxpayers' burden. Many so-called 'vagrants' were unemployed labourers moving around in search of work, perhaps unfairly penalised for using their initiative. There is no mention in the Sedgefield records of vagrants being admitted to the workhouse, although accounts report some given out-door relief.

Gaining admittance at all was difficult and discouraging methods used elsewhere may also have been adopted at Sedgefield Workhouse. People had to queue outside for entry, usually from 6pm, sometimes being doused with cold water for their pains. Workhouses often deliberately displayed a 'House Full' sign. Once inside, vagrants would be stripped of any valuables, their worth used to offset the cost of their owner's stay. This resulted in vagrants hiding possessions before attempting to gain admittance. Once inside the workhouse, they were stripped and bathed, often in cold water, and given grubby clothing to wear while their own clothes were 'stoved' to get rid of vermin. After spending the night in a primitive dormitory, often in coffin-like stalls, they had to perform tasks such as breaking stone before they were free to leave. In 1852, a uniform was adopted for all inmates although no description remains.

THE OLD WORKHOUSE

While the Poor Law Commission stipulated that the workhouse should be healthy and hygienic, with space adequate, conditions were to be no better than those enjoyed by the humblest of labourers. Since many labourers lived amidst squalor and degradation, the standard would have been easily achieved. The aim was to deter those who merely desired a comfortable bed for a few nights. Sedgefield's original workhouse, an old dilapidated building, stood in the east end of the town, near the present day East Well Farm. While the Guardians fought a ceaseless battle to maintain the fabric of the old building, over the years, ever mindful of the need to save money, they ignored countless request and reminders from London that accommodation be upgraded and improved. However, the inspectors continued, in common with all workhouses, to visit Sedgefield twice a year, reiterating the same requests each time. Sleeping accommodation for women and girls needed expanding, since the available area only just sufficed for present numbers. Any increase would lead to serious overcrowding. Despite such criticisms, for a long time, no improvements occurred, perhaps suggesting the central authorities were prepared to accept poor conditions, a deterrent to potential inmates.

Eventually, in an effort to cure the problem of dampness in ground floor quarters allocated to men, floors were replaced in two rooms. The women's yard, however, still suffered from an open drain 'into which filth of all sorts is thrown and from which a horrible smell emanated'. Materials to pave the yard had been lying there for a considerable time, constantly tripping up paupers, proving to be a real hazard. The composite material lining the women's day room was gradually breaking up, leaving large holes that filled with water in damp weather. The infirmary arrangements were most inadequate, the female sick bay a small room, only big enough to hold two beds and opening directly from the yard. The men were provided with even less. Sedgefield was asked to remedy the situation straight away.

The women's yard of a workhouse (c. 1840)

Sedgefield Guardians continued to receive letters from London encouraging an improvement to workhouse accommodation for almost twenty years, until, in 1854, they finally sent plans for the upgrading of the existing workhouse. However, in view of the amount of work involved, the Central Authorities suggested a completely new workhouse would be a better solution, a more costly proposal which was ignored by the Guardians. Since the workhouse was rarely full, they saw no reason for expansion, which they seemed to consider in terms of quantity of space, rather than quality of accommodation.

Difficulties arose in tracing the owner of the workhouse, for which the churchwardens had paid a peppercorn rent since its foundation. Work could not proceed without permission from the trustees. After much searching, in November 1856 clerk Richard Middleton reported that the Poor House, along with a piece of land called the 'White Bread Field', was originally bought with money left to the parish for the benefit of the poor of Sedgefield by a certain Mr Harrison. As such, the title of the property lay with a group of trustees, only one of whom was still alive. As any attempt to unravel the legal wrangle would be arduous, the subject was dropped, but the Poor Law Inspector responsible for Sedgefield continued to request a new workhouse on every visit.

THE NEW WORKHOUSE

In September, 1859, the Guardians reported that they had, at long last, begun the process of providing a new workhouse. In February 1860, Middleton reported a piece of land selected on the outskirts of the village, the area now known as Station Road. The building would house 60 inmates with wards, yards and other conveniences 'suitable for a complete classification'. Indicating the classes of pauper most likely to have recourse to the workhouse, twelve places would be available for men infirm through age or other causes and able-bodied men above sixteen. There would also be eighteen beds for infirm women and women over sixteen, ten for boys aged seven to sixteen and the same for girls. Finally ten places would be provided for children under seven and the sick and infectious.

As well as dormitory accommodation, there were to be detached rooms for vagrants of both sexes, a board-room for thirty guardians, a clerk's office, a waiting room, accommodation for the master and matron, a dining room for all and work rooms and dormitories for the boys and girls. Sleeping accommodation would provide 500 cubic feet of space for each inmate where rooms were occupied day and night, and 300 cubic feet in rooms used at night only. There would be a well in the able-bodied men's yard with a pump, cisterns provided with cold water, an underground rain-tank, lavatories, open fires and a good system of ventilation. The new workhouse would be brick built, at a cost of approximately £1,500.

The plans were sent off to London, but it was not long before adverse comments came back. First, it was noted that there was no accommodation for a porter, although the Commissioners added that a porter might not be needed for such a small house. A more serious concern, was that the plans showed the infectious wards communicating with the general kitchen and dining hall, with an obvious risk of the spread of infection. These wards should be constructed entirely separately, with their own yard, and should contain a nurse's room and bathroom. It was also pointed out that the plans contained no mention of a laundry. The windows of the dining hall, next to the men's yard, should be glazed with opaque glass in order to prevent men looking through on to the women's yard and vice versa. The windows of the day room were to be similarly treated. The walls round the exercise yard were to be eight feet high It was suggested there be two receiving wards, not just one, as the sexes had to be kept separate at all times. A blunder in the siting of the dead-house would involve removal of a corpse through the main building. Lastly, it was recommended that a refractory cell be constructed, measuring about ten feet by six feet, in a place where inmates could not communicate with the person contained within.

By the time all the suggested changes had been implemented and work was ready to begin, estimated costs had risen to £1,975, with an additional £300 for the land. The Guardians secured a loan, with an interest rate of 41.2% a year. In June 1861, Middleton reported that the money had run

The Workhouse in later years when it was used as an old people's home and known as Ivy House
(photo courtesy of Dave Nicholson)

out and a further £350 was needed. Bad weather, non availability of materials and mismanagement by the builder in charge had all led to delays. However, on 14th December 1861, the commissioners received a report that inmates had moved in three weeks previously, finding the new workhouse 'convenient and well arranged'. 24 years had elapsed since an inspector had first commented on the dire state of the old workhouse. The workhouse was extended in 1878 to accommodate 120 paupers and by the end of the century, each adult in the parish had to pay a rate of 3 shillings 4½ pence towards its maintenance. Much admired as a purpose-built institution, the new workhouse continued to stand until the 1990s when, despite a preservation order, it was deemed unsafe and demolished, having spent some intervening time as an old people's home, known as Ivy House.

MASTER AND MATRON

The Master and Matron had most dealings with the paupers once they entered the workhouse, supervising day to day running, determining matters such as diet and discipline, and deciding upon policies which deterred the poor from entering. Considered lower in status than other workhouse officials, more on a par with a modest tradesman, the Master, often a retired military man or policeman, poorly educated and with no training for the post, often struggled to deal with paperwork. From 1837 till 1859 Sedgefield's Master and Matron, William and Margaret Hallimond, lived at the workhouse with their daughter Jane. In 1845, various charges maliciously brought against the Master by two inmates included withholding food, not allowing paupers out to seek work, keeping his grandchild in the workhouse, stealing potatoes from the stores and being drunk. Government Inspector William Hawley vindicated the Master on all counts, pronouncing Sedgefield Workhouse in a 'state of greatest order and cleanliness'. When the Hallimonds retired, due to 'advanced years and infirmity', John Newton and his wife Mary were appointed Master and Matron of the workhouse. Judged more efficient than the previous Master, his salary was increased to £25 per annum, a fee still considerably below that of other officers.

THE MEDICAL OFFICER

When the Poor Law Union was set up in Sedgefield, the Board of Guardians appointed a Medical Officer to deal with the outdoor sick. In common with other appointments, the main consideration was how little could be paid to such a person. Although other officers received a salary, albeit a small one, the position of Medical Officer was put out to tender, the successful applicant being obliged to provide bandages and medicines out of his salary. Although the principle behind this was to ensure the paupers were not pampered by the overuse of medicines, it also meant that Medical Officers, often inexperienced young men just starting a career, found themselves out of pocket. Although the Guardians felt that the prestige of the position was sufficient reward, many discontented, underpaid and overworked doctors soon became severe critics of the workhouse system.

In 1842, school teacher Richard Lockey, passing on the opinion of many Sedgefield rate payers, suggested to the Commissioners in London that the system of tendering be replaced by a scale of charges for various treatments, applicable nationwide. The Union could then appoint a Medical Officer on merit rather than cheapness. Once agreed, the position of Medical Officer became much sought after, although Guardians continued to exploit doctors agreeable to taking on workhouse appointments at a very low salary. Rival doctors were thus kept out, while the Guardians' patronage would also assist young doctors in building up their own private practice. Only those who failed to establish a private practice would consider becoming Poor Law Doctors, the position carrying some loss of prestige.

In 1842, the Poor Law commissioners decreed that no medical man could be employed by the Guardians unless he had at least two of the recognised medical qualifications available at the time. Formerly, the Guardians had been at liberty to employ people with no qualifications at all. Although this stipulation did not entirely remove unqualified men, it helped lay the foundations for a truly professional body. In 1844, Sedgefield's current Medical Officer, Dr Slater, announced his intention not to continue in the post, as he did not consider the salary of £14 a year adequate. Shortly afterwards, the salary was raised to £20, exclusive of vaccination fees, and Dr Henry Ruddock appointed.

WORKHOUSE, INFIRMARY OR ASYLUM?

Due to the wide range of ailments suffered by its inmates, the workhouse resembled an infirmary, accepting people with a range of problems, mainly medical, that could not be catered for elsewhere. The institution housed the chronically sick, the incurable, the dying, the insane, expectant and nursing mothers, as well as those whose life of neglect had caused a variety of medical problems, some minor but nevertheless needing attention. Struggling with low wages and bureaucracy, most early officers employed in this multi-purpose institution acted as warders of the poor, rather than healers or attendants.

At first, medical relief formed a small part of the duties of Poor Law Officers, considered unimportant in comparison to outdoor relief. However, as the Government became more aware of the causes of diseases and methods of treatment, Poor Law officers acquired duties in the field of preventative medicine. In fact, later in the century, medical aspects of poor relief reached out to the whole community, so that, as well as sick paupers, the service cared for general public health. Because any epidemic or general malaise increased the burden on the poor rate, Guardians entrusted with this medical role could act in the general interest to maintain the health of the population. However, just as many people would rather starve than accept workhouse relief, whether indoor or outdoor, a similar stigma attached to the receipt of medical attention from the same source.

THE STIGMA OF VACCINATION

In 1840, Poor Law Unions were given responsibity for vaccination against smallpox. Boards were allowed to use discretion in deciding how this was to be carried out, either by a Medical Officer or, in smaller areas, a local practitioner, the option chosen at Sedgefield. Although the act applied to everyone, not just the poor, administration was to be borne by the poor rate, immediately attracting the stigma of charity. Consequently many people would not consider making use of it. The Commissioners suggested that the sum of 1 shilling and 6 pence be paid for every case but Sedgefield fixed their rate at 1 shilling. When surgery and midwifery rates were introduced in 1842, many Boards considered that their Medical Officers were now too highly paid, reducing their salaries accordingly.

By the 1850s, the low take up of vaccination had become a matter of national concern. On 27th October, 1852, in a letter presumably repeated nationwide, the Commissioners reminded Sedgefield Guardians of the prevalence of smallpox in the county and its increased mortality rate. The Guardians were urged to encourage local people to overcome their prejudice against a remedy provided by the Poor Law Union, emphasising the serious nature of smallpox and reminding the public that the service was free.

INSANITY

By the mid 19th century, while medical practice was becoming more specialised, to the good of the profession as a whole, Poor Law doctors continued to cover all aspects of medical care, although they could not hope to become experts in all areas. Few doctors, for instance, were expert in the treatment of insanity. However, the workhouse doctor was obliged to commit to the asylum any insane pauper considered dangerous. In less severe cases, he could follow his own judgement or the wishes of the Guardians, who were responsible for the costs of any pauper placed in an asylum. In order to save public money, insane paupers, even at a dangerous stage, often remained in the workhouse. Medical Officers were also pressured to reclassify sick paupers as fit, since illness entitled inmates to an enriched, more expensive diet.

As time went on, although workhouses were expected increasingly to care for the sick and the weak, few possessed appropriate accommodation. Successive Commissioners responsible for Sedgefield continually invoked the Guardians to consider building a sick ward, but not until the opening of the new workhouse in 1861 did accommodation for sick paupers reach a standard that met with the Commissioner's approval.

DIET

Since diet represented a major deterrent to entering the workhouse, the fare provided was plain and monotonous, although much better than many paupers were used to. As very little was known of nutrition, commissioners used the typical diet of a working man as a guide, regardless of its nutritional content. Anything that would have made the diet more palatable was taken out; often salt was not allowed on the table. Paupers were supplied with more bread than normally eaten by a labourer. Although criticised by many for its roughness, modern opinion would regard workhouse bread as more healthy than the refined white variety bought by those with money. Often, however, the bread would be stale and inedible, having to be eaten dry.

Women and children benefited more from a workhouse diet than men, since in the outside world their needs would be met after those of the breadwinner. In the workhouse, while a fixed amount of food was guaranteed for all, the Master would aim for as good a bargain as possible by ordering inferior products. While no law existed against the adulteration of food it was carried out widely. It is not known whether this practice was followed in Sedgefield, but milk was likely to be skimmed and any butter of a very inferior quality.

Strict regulations included the publication of the diet sheet for all to see, in case there was any cause for complaint. Diets were graded according to age and sex, the able-bodied receiving the plainest food in order to discourage them from entering the workhouse. The diet provided for inmates of Sedgefield was superior in many ways to that experienced by paupers in the south of England, where bread and cheese or bread and gruel were standard fare. Oatmeal porridge and broth, both provided at Sedgefield, would appear to be a slight step-up on the nutritional ladder from the insipid sounding gruel. Inmates at Sedgefield received one and a quarter pints of gruel for breakfast with six ounces of bread. Meat was served twice a week, making a third appearance in the form of ox-head stew or suet pudding on another. On a non-meat day, inmates were given one and a quarter pints of soup or one pint of rice and milk.

While this diet would provide sufficient energy, protein and minerals, paupers had a very low intake of Vitamins A and C, supplied only by potatoes plus vegetables added to broth. As a result, it is highly likely that inmates suffered from various deficiency diseases such as scurvy (lack of vitamin C), rickets (lack of vitamin D) and night blindness (lack of vitamin A). Unfortunately, no medical records are available to show what state these paupers were in. The diet of children, similarly deficient in vitamins, included one pint of milk a day. In those days, working class families did not drink milk, its nutritional value in terms of calcium content not being widely known.

CATEGORIES OF INMATE

The number of workhouse inmates varied according to the season, averaging at 22. In contrast to the biggest category, elderly infirm men, there were only ever a few women of this type. Old and infirm men were often left by their families to the mercies of the workhouse, whereas women in the same state often stayed with their families as child-minders. Often the next highest category, able-bodied women, were frequently young women with children who, having suffered a trauma such as desertion or widowhood, due to the burden of a young family, were unable to cope without assistance.

Few paupers were found amongst boys aged nine to sixteen, since they preferred to fend for themselves, rather than suffer the indignity of entering the workhouse. Children under the age of two only spent half their time with their mothers in the workhouse, the rest with a 'minder' in the village. Nothing is known of the type of care they would receive there. Numerous unmarried pregnant women, some just girls, came into the workhouse for anything up to a few months before the birth or sometimes only days, staying perhaps for several months. Their babies did not appear to stay full-time in the workhouse, spending one day in, one day out during the week, suggesting some form of foster care

A PAUPER FAMILY

Reasons for admission, listed by each pauper in the Admissions and Discharge Book, often very illuminating, cast a great deal of light upon the social situations of many inmates. Along with occasional mention of husbands being transported, females frequently reported 'husband in prison' and 'deserted by husband and/or father'. Details of the Cunningham family, for instance, indicate the multitude of functions carried out by the workhouse, often imperfectly, due to untrained staff and inadequate facilities. For the Cunninghams, as for countless others, the workhouse served, both in the short and long term, as a shelter for the unemployed, a refuge for battered wives and neglected children, a maternity home, a hospital and a lunatic asylum.

The Admission and Discharge Registers of Sedgefield Workhouse show that, between 1840 and 1849, Honor Cunningham, deserted by her husband, 25 years her senior, frequently stayed in the workhouse, often for short periods, with her five children, three of whom were born there. When, in 1846, her four year old son Robert was taken ill, he stayed in the workhouse alone for two weeks to recover. Husband Robert returned occasionally, but was violent, abusive and mentally unstable.

In 1848, when the whole family were living in the workhouse, Mrs Cunningham, discharged by the Guardians for 'being disorderly and misbehaved', was sent to prison for fourteen days, along with her baby son John. Although no details of either offence are recorded, husband Robert was imprisoned days later for a similar term. Their children stayed in the workhouse. The following year, young Robert and his sister Mary, aged seven and ten, deserted by their mother, were admitted to the workhouse. As the children grew older, although still very young by modern standards, they sought independence from their inadequate parents and disappear from workhouse records.

Father Robert, however, deteriorated, his mental health increasingly unstable. After several short spells alone in the workhouse, he stayed for a longer period between June 1855 and January 1856, at which point he was imprisoned for six months. After Robert's return to the workhouse, the Commissioner for Lunacy who had just made an inspection at Sedgefield, reported thus '…*lately imprisoned for six months for a severe assault on another inmate and placed on the list of the insane since his discharge from gaol. He has conducted himself quietly since his return but considering the great lack of supervision for this class of inmate, he should be carefully watched and removed to an asylum if he causes any bother'*. Imprisoned for a further nine months in January 1858, for violent and abusive conduct towards the medical officer, Robert Cunningham then returned to the workhouse. After serving another jail term in 1860, he died in 1863 aged 74.

In 1857, William Hurst of the Poor Law Commissioners, deploring the acute shortage of space at Sedgefield Workhouse, cited as an example that Robert Cunningham 'while mad' was obliged to be locked up in a cupboard with the pots and kettles. He had earlier suggested, in 1856, that Robert *'while not a dangerous lunatic is still a man of such mischievous propensities that he ought not to remain in the workhouse unless some special provision be made by the Guardians for his separate accommodation'*. Although records frequently describe workhouse inmates being of 'unsound mind' or 'mentally defective', only the worst cases were transferred to a mental hospital or asylum. Others were given shelter, the minimum of attention and allowed to exist in a state of apathy.

In January 1847, Sedgefield Guardians, listing their mentally ill paupers during the last quarter, with only ten inmates resident, described six as 'lunatics' or 'idiots'. Two more 'lunatics' supported by the Poor Law lived with relatives. Two inmates were described as not dangerous, one, aged 22, a danger to himself, while two were considered most definitely dangerous - a 36 year old woman, insane since the age of 17 months, and a 63 year old man insane since childhood. No treatment was provided. These inmates sat around all day staring at the wall. A visiting Assistant Commissioner commented favourably on their 'docile' nature, finding them in a 'tranquil and comfortable state and apparently quite tractable and harmless'.

THE SEDGEFIELD CHARITIES

For a place of its size, Sedgefield possessed a remarkable number of charities. A report by the Parish Council of 1897 listed 25, the earliest beginning in 1630. They were classified under six headings - School Endowments, Almshouses, Lamb's Charity, Money Dole, Bread Dole and Apprentices.

Cooper's Almshouses not long before they were demolished in the 1960s
(photo by kind permission of the late Joyce Wilkinson)

School Endowments, with a total annual value in 1895 of £49 15 shillings 8 pence, included various bequests such as those of John Lowther, Richard Wright and Mrs Strong's gift of the school. In May 1885, in a thorough report on Sedgefield Charities, the Northern Echo recorded London merchant William Soulaby's bequest of £300 to the church wardens and trustees of the old Grammar School. The Master would receive interest in perpetuity to provide education for two poor children between the ages of 7 and 10, to be instructed in Latin and the classics up to the age of 14.

In 1702, Thomas Cooper bequeathed £100 to build 10 almshouses for 5 poor men and 5 poor women over 50 living in Sedgefield. The people, who would also be paid £2 half yearly, were to be nominated by the Rector and 24 of the parish. Each would receive a blue coat, value 8 shillings, the sleeves bearing the initials TC in yellow. Anyone refusing to wear the uniform would be disqualified from entering the almshouses, the cost of repairs for which would be borne equally by each recipient. Tenants could not have anyone living with them, except in case of sickness. If there were

Examples of poorer dwellings in Sedgefield – these were near the junction of Station Road and West Park Lane. (photo courtesy of Joyce Wilkinson)

not enough poor in Sedgefield to fill the spaces, the deficiency was to be made up with poor from Cornforth. The annual income of Cooper's Almshouses was £142 18 shillings 4 pence and each inmate received £14 5 shillings 10 pence per annum. By the second half of the century the Almshouses were in a bad state of repair, but in 1868 were restored, the cost raised by public subscription. By 1895, the provision of a coat for each inhabitant had been discontinued, the value of 8 shillings given in lieu.

Although very much reduced in value in modern times, the Sedgefield Charities still exist in a combined form today, available to help needy students with further education.

A rather indestinct photo showing the view down Front Street with the Cooper's Almshouses on the right
(photo courtesy of Dave Nicholson)

CHAPTER 15 EVENTS OUTSIDE SEDGEFIELD

The Victorian era was far more cosmopolitan than generally imagined. Victorian Sedgefield was by no means an isolated community, nor were its inhabitants exclusively Sedgefield born. The increasing availability of newspapers meant that, as well as matters of local interest, people could be well informed about national and international affairs. Often couched in fulsome language, articles were avidly devoured by the more literate members of the public, who craved information.

Famous for lurid reportage of all kinds, including crime, scandal and warfare, the Victorian press did not lack material, as Queen Victoria's reign witnessed numerous landmark events. Local papers, the Darlington and Stockton Times, founded in 1847, and the Northern Echo, first printed on 1 January 1870, reported on events all over the globe.

HOME AND AWAY

Very close to home, the main event reported on 20 February 1882, a mining disaster, the Trimdon Grange Explosion, resulted in the deaths of 70 men and boys. Although no one from Sedgefield died, the disaster would have been keenly felt in the village, just a few miles away from Trimdon Grange, possibly home to relatives of Sedgefield people.

From the other side of the world, an article in the Darlington and Stockton Times of 6 January 1849 must have caught many an eye, reporting on *'The Gold of California'*. *'Five hundred square miles in California abound with gold in every yard of its expanse, the soil being impregnated with it in a great abundance so as to require but digging up and washing to yield its wealth'*. There is no record of whether any Sedgefield people were enticed to try their luck after reading such an article, but it is well known that thousands from all over the world flocked to California for the 'Gold Rush', few making any money from the experience.

A town named to honour 19th century South African politician and industrialist, Henry Barrington, is a long way from his birthplace Sedgefield, Co. Durham. Actions by Barrington's offspring led indirectly to the naming of Sedgefield, West Cape.

The memorial for Crimean War soldier Frederick Hardwicke Bolton in Sedgefield graveyard. (LHS archive)

WAR REPORTING

By the middle of 1854, much press attention focused on the Crimean war, the first to be reported so swiftly after events happened. The invention of telegraphy and the presence of reporters in the field meant that each military action was reported in great detail. There was, therefore, great joy in Sedgefield and beyond when allied troops began the siege of Sebastopol in October, 1854, eventually leading to the defeat of the Russians. In Sedgefield churchyard stands a memorial to Frederick Hardwicke Bolton, a 21 year old sergeant in the Sixth Iniskilling Dragoon Guards, who fell in the charge of the Heavy Brigade at the Battle of Balaclava on 25 October, 1854.

According to the Darlington and Stockton Times of the time *'the Iniskilling and Scot's Greys pierced through the dark masses of the Russians. There was a clash of steel and a light play of sword blades in the air, and then the Greys and the Redcoats disappeared into the thick of the shaken and quivering columns. .. In another moment we saw them emerging and dashing on in diminished numbers, and in broken order, against the second line'*. It was probably in this action that Sergeant Bolton met his death. Later the same day, the Light Brigade suffered terrible losses when famously dispatched 'under imbecile command'. In the cemetery of the former Winterton Hospital, on the outskirts of Sedgefield, lies the grave of John Nichol, who died on 3 November, 1893 after serving the previous 18 years as chief attendant at the Asylum. A bugler in the Fourth Royal Irish Dragoon Guards, he took part in the charge of the Heavy Brigade at Balaclava.

By 1857, newspapers were reporting in great detail the atrocities of the Indian Mutiny. By the end of 1899, the international event preoccupying the press was the Boer War, referred to at the time as the 'Transvaal War'. Mr Ralph Ord, JP presided at a meeting in the Parish Hall which agreed to raise money for the wives and families of serving soldiers, amongst them eight Sedgefield men, two of whom were about to depart for South Africa. Mr W. Gibbon and Mr T. Sotheran, both of the Princess of Wales Own York's regiment, were given a rousing send off at the Golden Lion Inn, where 'patriotic songs were sung', the health of the reservists drunk and 25 shillings and 6 pence collected for the Reservists Fund. Both men left the following morning, taking the 6 o'clock train for the barracks in

The charge of the Light Brigade by Richard Caton Woodville (1825-55)

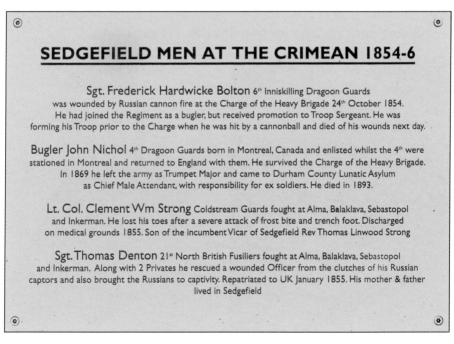

SEDGEFIELD MEN AT THE CRIMEAN 1854-6

Sgt. Frederick Hardwicke Bolton 6th Inniskilling Dragoon Guards
was wounded by Russian cannon fire at the Charge of the Heavy Brigade 24th October 1854.
He had joined the Regiment as a bugler, but received promotion to Troop Sergeant. He was
forming his Troop prior to the Charge when he was hit by a cannonball and died of his wounds next day.

Bugler John Nichol 4th Dragoon Guards born in Montreal, Canada and enlisted whilst the 4th were
stationed in Montreal and returned to England with them. He survived the Charge of the Heavy Brigade.
In 1869 he left the army as Trumpet Major and came to Durham County Lunatic Asylum
as Chief Male Attendant, with responsibility for ex soldiers. He died in 1893.

Lt. Col. Clement Wm Strong Coldstream Guards fought at Alma, Balaklava, Sebastopol
and Inkerman. He lost his toes after a severe attack of frost bite and trench foot. Discharged
on medical grounds 1855. Son of the incumbent Vicar of Sedgefield Rev Thomas Linwood Strong

Sgt. Thomas Denton 21st North British Fusiliers fought at Alma, Balaklava, Sebastopol
and Inkerman. Along with 2 Privates he rescued a wounded Officer from the clutches of his Russian
captors and also brought the Russians to captivity. Repatriated to UK January 1855. His mother & father
lived in Sedgefield

Plaque to the Sedgefield participants in the Crimean War, just outside Sedgefield Churchyard

Richmond. About a week later, Theresa, Lady Londonderry visited the homes of the two men plus that of a Mr Murphy, indicating her intention to send them a sum of 6 shillings and 6 pence each week, adding that, if that was not enough, she was to be informed. The Northern Echo reported that 'the noble lady was warmly thanked by the parties concerned'.

POLITICS

Politics, also of great interest to many, received extensive press coverage. In April, 1857, at a General Election, the Constituency elected its two Members of Parliament, Lord Harry Vane and Henry Pease. A previous incumbent, James Farrer esquire, was voted out. In those days, no privacy was attached to elections, since a list published of all constituency electors also indicated their choice of candidate. In 1868, the Northern Chronicle reported Mr W. Arbuthnot, radical parliamentary candidate for Gateshead, presently residing at Hardwick Hall, would support both W.E. Gladstone and John Bright as leaders of the Liberal party. In 1890, the Northern Echo reported on the rise of liberalism in Sedgefield. A well attended public meeting held at the Mechanics' Institute under the auspices of the Durham Liberal association heard a lecture, 'Ireland under Balfour'. Illustrated by magic lantern slides, the talk considered plans for giving Home Rule to Ireland.

William Ewart Gladstone (1809 -98) - one of Britains's longest serving politicians

Lord Harry Vane, 4th Duke of Cleveland, MP for South Durham from 1841 – 59

The Royal Wedding of Princess Victoria Mary of Teck to the Duke of York, later George V. (7th July, 1893)

Prince Albert who died in 1861 by Franz Xavier Winterhalter

ROYALTY

In December, 1861 newspapers were full of dismay at the early death of Prince Albert, husband of Queen Victoria. In March, 1863, they covered the marriage of the Prince of Wales to Princess Alexandra of Denmark, an event celebrated with festivities all over the country. July 1893 saw the marriage of Prince George, eldest son of the Prince of Wales to Princess May (as Princess Victoria was familiarly known) of Teck, the couple later to become King George V and Queen Mary. As usual, the people of Sedgefield took the opportunity to celebrate an event of national importance. The Northern Echo reported that Canon and Mrs Falconer invited 500 children and old people to tea at the Rectory, followed by foot racing, pony racing, barrow and pole climbing. Workhouse inmates were treated to 'special fayre', including many gallons of beer courtesy of Mr Forster of Bishop Middleham. The day finished with a display of fireworks.

CHAPTER 16
THE LAST YEAR OF VICTORIAN ENGLAND

As the century turned and the last year of Victoria's reign began, life in Sedgefield continued as normal, with the usual run of social events and meetings. In January, Sedgefield Town Football club, reportedly doing well, were busy organising a social in the Parish Hall. In March 1900, a good deal of excitement followed the news that roads were to be put into good repair in readiness for motor car trials, soon to take place on the 'main road', possibly the main road north at Rushyford. Yet again, health matters were prominent, a good deal of worry concerning the current epidemic of influenza. People were warned to beware of 'quacks' trying to sell potions and pills, not just for influenza but all sorts of illnesses. The Northern Echo of the time was full of adverts for a so-called 'miracle pill'.

The same variations of weather occurred as usual, local newspapers displaying the normal British preoccupation with meteorological matters. There was a terrific storm in late October of 1900 with really strong gales. For miles, south of Sedgefield, lay a 'huge sheet of water of no inconsiderable depth with just the tops of the trees visible'. Many sheep and cattle had suffered.

The main international event, the Transvaal War, now known as the Boer War, continued to be reported every day in the newspapers. Due to the invention of telegraph, for the first time, the population could be informed of events such as the siege of Mafeking and Ladysmith almost as soon as they happened. However, the press also made people aware of many military blunders committed, as well as the British invention of a system of concentration camps, created to deal with the wives and families of their Boer opponents. Many were to die in squalid conditions there.

THE ROYAL FAMILY
In April 1900, while the Prince of Wales was in Brussels en route to Denmark, an attempt was made on his life by an assailant, who jumped onto the footplate of his train. Fortunately, the man was soon caught. Queen Victoria, despite her advancing years remained very busy. In the

Queen Victoria in her later years

early months of 1900, she made a lengthy official visit to Ireland. By the start of 1901, however, newspapers were reporting anxiety about her health. She was now spending all her time at Osborne House on the Isle of Wight. After speculation that she would be too unwell to take her forthcoming continental holiday, by 22nd January the worst was feared. Members of the Royal family, including the Queen's grandson, the Kaiser of Germany, were summoned to her bedside. She died later that day. The following morning, the Northern Echo, edged in black, devoted almost the entire issue to reportage of the Queen's death and articles about her life. She died at the age of 81, having ruled for 63 years over a nation and an Empire that had seen many rapid changes.

The funeral procession of Queen Victoria showing the new King Edward VII and the German Kaiser following the coffin.

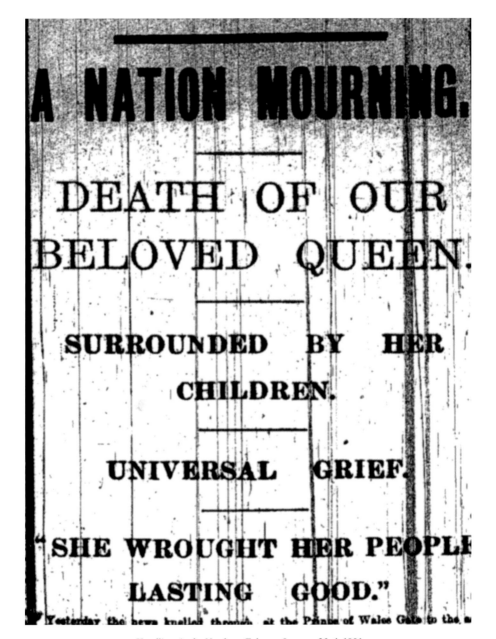

Headlines in the Northern Echo on January 23rd, 1901

BIBLIOGRAPHY

The Story of our Village
– Elizabeth Dunn (Sedgefield Women's Institute)

Charity Commissioners' reports relating to Sedgefield

Sedgefield Census reports 1841 – 1901

Behind the Wall. The life and times of Winterton Hospital
– Adam Lamb and Jack Turton.

Sedgefield, a social and Historical Miscellany - compiled by members of an evening class on Sedgefield's local history (WEA)

The Reawakening of Hardwick Park, Sedgefield – the Friends of Hardwick Park.

The History and Antiquities of the County Palatine of Durham
– William Hutchinson

The History and Antiquities of the County Palatine of Durham
– Robert Surtees

The History and Antiquities of the County Palatine of Durham
– William Fordyce (1857)

The Victoria History of County Durham

History, Topography and Directory of the County Palatine of Durham – 1894

The County Books, Durham – Sir Timothy Eden

The Sedgefield Country in the 80s and 90s – William Dresser (1904)

The Darlington and Stockton Times

The Newcastle Courant

The Northern Echo

The Care of the Poor in Sedgefield 1837-1861
– Alison Hodgson (MA dissertation 1990)